QUICK-QUILTED

Home Decor

WITH

YOUR SEWING MACHINE

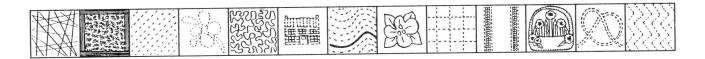

OTHER BOOKS AVAILABLE FROM CHILTON
Robbie Fanning, *Series Editor*

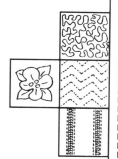

Home Decor

WITH

YOUR SEWING MACHINE

JACKIE DODSON

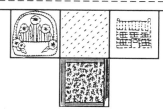

CONTEMPORARY
QUIL*TING

CHILTON BOOK COMPANY
Radnor, Pennsylvania

Designed by Stanley S. Drate / Folio Graphics Co. Inc.

Packaged by March Tenth, Inc.

Manufactured in the United States of America

Library of Congress Cataloging in Publication Data

Dodson, Jackie.
    Quick-quilted home decor with your sewing machine/Jackie Dodson.
      p.   cm. — (Contemporary quilting)
    Includes bibliographical references and index.
    ISBN 0-8019-8368-1 (pbk.)
    1. Machine quilting — Patterns.   2. House furnishings.   3. Interior
decoration — Amateurs' manuals. I. Title. II. Series.
TT835.D64   1993
746.9 — dc20   93-30048
                                                    CIP

1 2 3 4 5 6 7 8 9 0   2 1 0 9 8 7 6 5 4 3

Trade Names and Registered Trademarks used in this book:

Aleene's Stop Fraying	Pearls N Piping
Craft Cord	Pellon
Fasturn	Radio Shack
Fiskars	Sulky
Gingher	Tandy
HeatnBond	Teflon
Household Goop	ThreadFuse
Hump Jumper	Ultrasuede
Lily's Sugar 'n' Cream	Velcro
Masonite	Waist Shaper
Mundial	Wonder Under

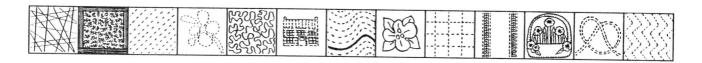

CONTENTS

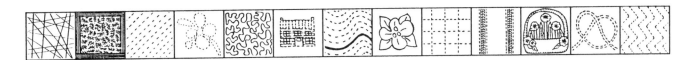

CHAPTER 3

Bedroom   64

CHAPTER 4

Quilting/Sewing Shortcuts   82

CHAPTER 5

What Size Will It Be?   89

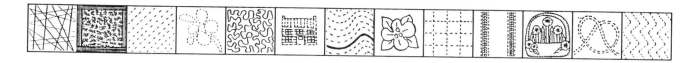

FOREWORD

My neighbor came to the door today. I was in the middle of editing this book. She was wearing an attractive black T-shirt crisscrossed by diagonal bands of bias tape in primary colors. In some areas, a patch of tape hung free, about three inches long and knotted.

I stared in amazement. "Look!" I said and held up Jackie Dodson's Reversible Pillow Top, Project 4 in Chapter 1. It is squares of black chintz crisscrossed by bias tape in bright colors, surrounded by a fringe of knotted bias tape.

This is what I love about all of Jackie's books. I learned a technique for gathering strips in *Twenty Easy Machine-Made Rugs*—and now I can use it in smaller scale for texture on a garment. I learned how to use the various presser feet in *Know Your Sewing Machine*, and now I have the tools to sew anything.

That's an invaluable gift.

ROBBIE FANNING
Series Editor

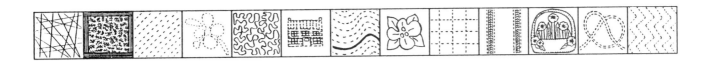

ACKNOWLEDGMENTS

Thank you:

To my mother, Kap Hanson, who showed me what fun it is to make something out of nothing. To my aunt, Helen Ove, whose hands and mind were always creating, and my aunt, Fritz Martin, whose home is an inspiration of hand-made, house beautiful.

To Sue Hausmann and Viking/White Sewing Machine Co. for always having the answers when I ask.

To JoAnn Pugh, Kathy Embry, Sharon Kelly, and Bernina of America, who come to my aid whenever I call them.

To Jan Saunders, for listening, advising, and being on the same wavelength.

To Marilyn Tisol and Nancy Bednar, a special friend, critic, and sounding board.

And to my editor, Robbie Fanning, for her optimism, encouragement, and endless support.

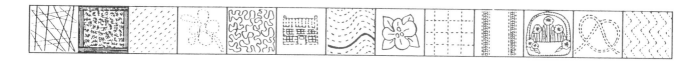

INTRODUCTION

Why would anyone spend time sewing home decorations when they can buy whatever they need? We all know the answer: Yes, we can buy what we *need*—but we can make what we *want*. There's a difference. For example, I needed curtains for a bedroom window—quick—when friends invited themselves for the weekend, so I decided to buy curtains (a first) mail-order, to save even more time. Well, they are what I *need* but certainly not what I *want*. When the curtains arrived, I hated the fabric and the skimpiness that was supposedly the right size but didn't come together in the middle without leaving the sides open; and the closest curtain length I could choose was either too long or too short. I still want to make curtains for that bedroom window.

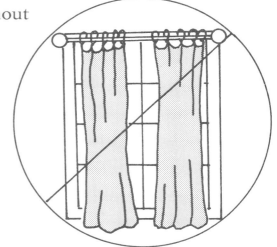

Here's what I *need,* not what I *want.* Let's stamp out curtains that don't fit.

More and more of us are finding that with new notions, fusibles, drapery tapes, and threads, along with teaching videos, sergers, miracle sewing machines, and gorgeous fabrics, we can custom-make beautiful home decorations quickly. And if we make them ourselves, they'll reflect our tastes, they'll fit, and the price will be right.

Why is there a trend to home decoration in sewing? A TV reporter had this answer: We are becoming burrowers. One reason for that is we feel safer at home than on the streets. We burrow when we rent videos instead of attending a movie, send out for pizza instead of eating in a restaurant, call a grocery store to deliver our food, mail-order instead of shop at the

9

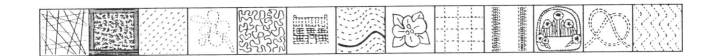

mall. More and more businesses are in the home. We don't have to go out of the house.

Gerald Calente, a trend researcher for the Socio-Economic Research Institute, claims that the recession is a cause for this stay-at-home attitude. We don't have the money to go out, so we stay at home.

It only follows that we want to beautify the surroundings where we spend most of our time. Whatever the reason, the fact remains that we are decorating our homes and doing it ourselves.

Fabric stores are taking the lead with their "home dec" departments, a term invented in the last couple of years. Today's store devotes more square feet to decorating the home than were there a year ago. Sample curtains, swags, and pillows tempt the do-it-yourselfer, along with new products, books, and pamphlets to help you decorate every inch of space in your home.

Of course, sewing and fabric catalogs offer everything needed for decorating (see "Sources of Supplies"), and they're delivered to our homes, so all we have to do is fill out an order, slip it into a mailbox, and go back to our burrows.

When you read through the projects, you'll discover that this book shows you how to decorate with machine-quilting; it's not a book to teach you how to machine-quilt. (If you want to learn machine-quilting basics, I suggest two Chilton books: *The Complete Book of Machine Quilting* by Robbie and Tony Fanning and *Teach Yourself Machine Piecing and Quilting* by Debra Wagner.)

When I burrow, I love to sew, and quilting by machine is one of my favorite activities. For the little time it takes to decorate with machine-quilting, the results are terrific.

The machine-sewn projects in this book are in Chapters 1, 2, and 3:

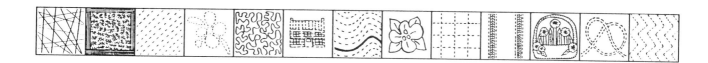

"Living Room," "Bathroom," and "Bedroom." The first decorative accessory I show you how to make is a flowered wallhanging, an example of the many ways to machine-quilt. Even if you don't make the wallhanging, try all the techniques and place the results in a notebook or on a bulletin board, where you can refer to them as you stitch the other projects.

In addition to the sampler are four other large, machine-quilted projects: summer quilt, shower curtain, bathroom rug, and tablecloth. Along with those 5 projects are 13 others that may or may not be quilted. They are added to coordinate and complement the other accessories in the three room settings. There is something for every taste. If you don't find yourself in one of them, it may take only a fabric change to make it truly you.

More information is included in size charts, a list of sources for supplies, and a bibliography of other home dec books to keep you busy the rest of your life.

I promised you *quick* quilting on the sewing machine. Check Chapter 4, "Shortcuts," to see how I cut down construction, as well as decorating, time. Use these tips and hints whenever applicable in all of your sewing.

This book is a collection of ideas I've played with through the years. Instead of leaving an experiment as only a square of stitching on my sewing table, I've used the ideas for projects, and now you have the benefit of some of those experiments. I'm always finding new threads, fabrics, glues, notions, and products that weren't here yesterday, so I feel I'll never finish experimenting.

Use the ideas in this book as I've shown them, or use them as a jumping-off place for your own experiments. I don't believe in always following directions, and I hope you approach the projects with that in mind. Change them to colors you like and use your favorite decorative stitches, threads, and methods. That's what makes your home look like you. It's also what makes sewing home decor fun.

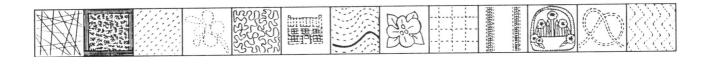

Pamela Clabburn from Norwich, England, defines quilting in *The Needleworker's Dictionary*: "The stitching together of two or three thicknesses of fabric to make something which can be warm, protective, or purely decorative." That definition can include appliqué, reverse appliqué, layering sheers and transparencies, and much more. It's fun to stretch the quilting imagination, so let's get to it.

CHAPTER 1

Living Room

The first of three room settings contains accessories suitable for a living room or bedroom.

In this setting, a tablecloth for a low 36″ (.95m) round tabletop reaches the floor and hides the table. Then, using the same colors as the flowered square in the cloth, I quilted a wallhanging sampler of machine-quilting techniques and added three quilted pillows. Two quick unquilted projects, a petticoat lampshade cover and and felt penny rug wallhanging, are also included.

Projects include: Machine-Quilted Sampler, Fool-the-Eye Tablecloth, Nine-Patch Pillow Top, Reversible Pillow Top, Yo-yo Basket Pillow, Petticoat Lampshade Cover, and Penny Rug Wallhanging.

Machine-Quilted Sampler

"Do you machine-quilt because it's faster?" is a question I'm often asked. Or someone may volunteer, "Of course you machine-quilt because you don't have time for hand-quilting." Somehow the idea that I machine-quilt because I enjoy it, or because the effects I want can't be accomplished by hand, escapes some people. It's a common belief that the reason one machine-quilts is because there's a lack of time, patience, or talent to hand-quilt. I hope the projects in this book show you that machine quilting is a

YOU WILL NEED:

Fabric: 1¼ yds. (1.14m) black chintz, for backing

8½″ × 7″ (21.6cm × 18cm) piece of gray/brick-red plaid chintz, for vase

15″ × 24″ (38cm × 61cm) black/white pin dot, for lower part of the background

19″ × 15″ (48.5cm × 38cm) gray/white striped chintz, for upper left-hand background area

19″ × 11″ (48.5cm × 28cm) rosebud and black print, for upper right-hand background area

¾ yd. (68.5cm) plain brick-red chintz, for flower petals

⅓ yd. (30.5cm) light green, for top area behind flowers

8″ (20.5cm) square of green print, for multi-stem design

1⅓ yds. (1.2m) striped fabric, for frame

Scraps of other green and yellow/green fabrics, and green pin dot, for leaves and stems

Green leaves and small flowers from tablecloth fabric (see Project 2)

Scraps of mauve chintz, for flower petals

1 yd. (.95m) black tulle, to stretch over collage

Needle: #90/14 jeans (sharp)

Thread: Smoke-colored monofilament; black sewing; green cotton and rose rayon machine-embroidery

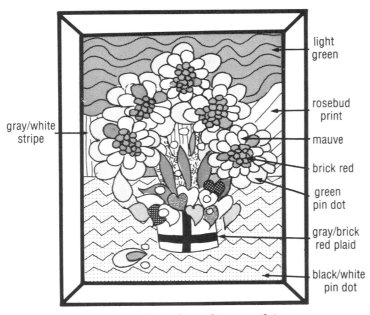

light green

rosebud print

mauve

brick red

green pin dot

gray/brick red plaid

black/white pin dot

gray/white stripe

1.1 ▪ **Sampler of machine-quilting.**

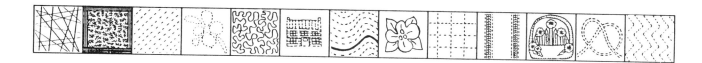

Presser feet: Embroidery; general purpose; zipper

Batting: 1 yd. × 1½ yds. (.95m × 1.4m) fusible fleece, for backing pin dot, striped, rosebud fabrics, and frame; handful of fiberfill

Miscellaneous: Paper-backed fusible web; silver quilting pencil; yard-stick; rotary cutter and mat; glue stick; quilting pins; 3 small plastic rings and dowel, for hanging (optional); 8 yds. (7.3m) of ¼" (6mm) cable cord

technique of its own. Yes, machine-quilting goes faster, but it isn't a clone of hand-quilting. It has its own personality and style, and machine-quilters are still experimenting and finding new ways to use it.

All machine-quilting is placed in one of two categories: stitching with feed dogs raised or stitching with feed dogs lowered or covered.

Included in the first category (feed dogs raised) is stitch-in-the-ditch, trapunto, Italian cording, sashiko, echoing, and stitching with decorative or straight stitches in straight or curved lines (see Figs. 1.2–1.7). The second category (called free-machine quilting) is accomplished with the feed dogs lowered or

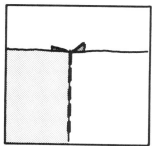

1.2 ▪ Stitch-in-the-ditch on top of a seam.

1.3 ▪ Pad area between quilting stitches to raise an area (trapunto).

1.4 ▪ Thread cord through a channel between a double row of stitches (Italian cording).

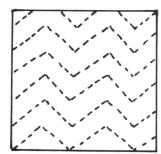

1.5 ▪ Stitch even rows of quilting for one type of sashiko (simple running stitches to hold layers of fabric together).

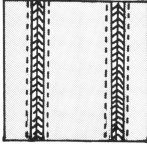

1.6 ▪ Embellish printed fabric with straight or decorative machine stitches.

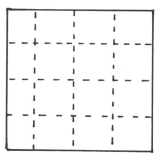

1.7 ▪ Stitch a sandwich of fabric and batting together with sewing-machine quilting.

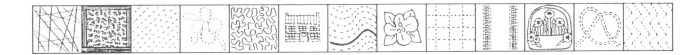

covered. It includes stippling, outlining, drawing, echoing, and trapunto (see Figs. 1.3, 1.8–1.11).

In the flowered wallhanging are examples of most of these techniques.

It doesn't look quick to you? Read through the directions first to discover how fast this can be sewn. I constructed the large hanging in three smaller sections, which I sewed together later. It's easier to work on smaller sections so it takes less time. Also, if a section has to be replaced because I've made a mistake too awful to rip out or cover up, it's far easier to replace a small section than it is the entire hanging. You'll discover, too, that exact patterns aren't used. Though I give you an idea of a shape, they are all cut out freehand.

Although I used a traditional satin stitch to appliqué parts of the hanging, most of the pieces in the bouquet of flowers are held in place by stretching bridal veil (black tulle) over the batting-backed picture. The petals and leaves are trapped between veil and background by stitching around them. What an easy, fast way to appliqué and quilt at the same time.

To coordinate the living room setting, I used the same chintz fabrics and color scheme on all projects in this chapter. The colors include black, mauve, blue, peach, yellow, green, ivory, and gray. I've added stripes, pin dots, and prints along with the plain fabrics.

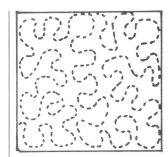

1.8 ▪ Stippling, quilting with feed dogs lowered, looks like jigsaw-puzzle cuts.

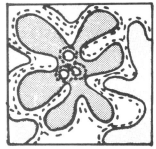

1.9 ▪ Free-quilting is effective when outlining designs in fabrics.

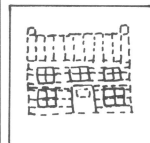

1.10 ▪ Quilt in your own designs.

1.11 ▪ Echo quilting a line in a design.

1.12 ▪ **Quilt striped fabric with both straight stitching and decorative machine-stitches.**

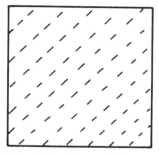

1.13 ▪ **Use lines of diagonal stitches to quilt the rosebud fabric.**

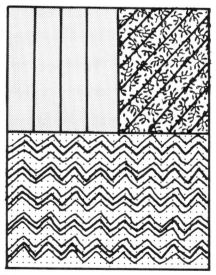

1.14 ▪ **Use jagged lines of sashiko at the bottom of the wallhanging.**

The finished picture, without frame, is 30″ × 22½″ (76cm × 57cm). It has a 4½″ (11.5cm) mitered border added around it.

Back the piece of gray-and-white striped chintz with fusible fleece. Fusible fleece is a 100%-polyester needle-punched fleece with a fusible backing (it eliminates basting and saves time). Use rose rayon thread to quilt lines of decorative stitches between stripes, and for lines of straight stitches at the sides of some stripes (Fig. 1.12). Put this aside.

Place the rosebud print on the table and draw diagonal lines, a yardstick's width apart, with a silver quilting pencil. Cover all the fabric with these lines. Back with fusible fleece, then straight-stitch on the marked lines, using black thread (Fig. 1.13).

Draw zigzag lines on the pin-dot fabric. These are approximately 1½″ (4cm) long on the diagonal and 1¾″ (4.5cm) high (Fig. 1.14). After backing the fabric with fusible fleece, stitch in a zigzag design, like sashiko. With black in the bobbin, to match the fabric, and the needle threaded with doubled rose rayon machine-embroidery thread or smoke monofilament thread, stitch the jagged lines with stitch length slightly longer than normal (stitch length 3). (I varied the thread color by stitching two lines with monofilament, then one row with rose thread. I followed this progression from the top to the bottom of the pin dot. Unlike a perfect sashiko, I skipped a line or two for variety.)

Assemble the three parts of the picture

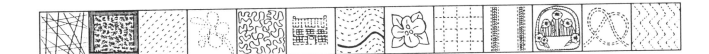

you have finished. To do this, fold under the right-hand side of the striped fabric and overlap the rosebud fabric. Sew beside the fold with a narrow blanket stitch, letting the short bite catch the fold as you progress. Finish assembling the background by folding under the top of the pin-dot fabric, placing it over the edge of the top fabrics, then stitching this in place with the same blanket stitch as before. All the stitching is practically invisible when accomplished with monofilament thread.

Back the light green fabric with fusible fleece and press. Cut the bottom edge in a free-form curving line. Place the fabric over the top 11″ (28cm) of the picture. Straight-stitch, with green cotton machine-embroidery thread, along the wavy edge. After smoothing out the fabrics, continue stitching the top of the picture in quilting lines spaced approximately ½″ (1.3cm) to 1½″ (4cm) apart, echoing the first curved line (Fig. 1.15). Satin-stitch (stitch width 3) over the straight stitches at the curved bottom edge.

Fold under ¼″ (6mm) of the sides and bottom edges of the plaid vase, after adding a brick-red strip of fabric across it (to visually add weight—see Fig. 1.1). Use rose satin stitches across the top and bottom edges of the strip.

Appliqué the vase to the sashiko piece as shown. Use a wide blanket stitch (stitch width 3) and black thread for a hand-appliquéd look.

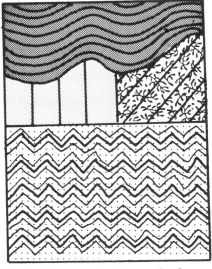

1.15 ▪ **Attach and echo-quilt the top area.**

1.16 ▪ **Cut out 9″ (23cm) leaves in this shape.**

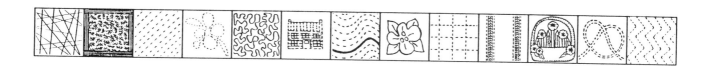

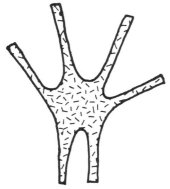

1.17 ▪ **Use this shape to fill in space between the vase and flowers.**

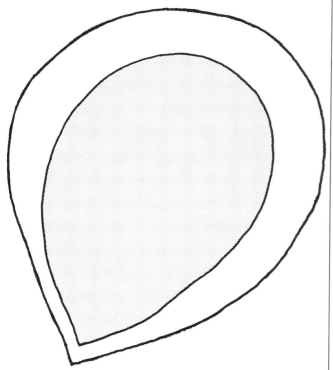

1.18 ▪ **This is the pattern for larger leaves and smaller petals.**

Back several colors of plain green and green print with fusible web. No pattern is needed to cut out four 9″ × 1″ (23cm × 2.5cm) leaves (Fig. 1.16) and four ½″ (1.3cm) stems the same length.

Cut out an 8″ (20.5cm) square of green print fabric and back it with fusible web. Then cut out a multi-stemmed design (Fig. 1.17), place it over the background on top of the vase, and press in place. Satin-stitch (stitch width 2) with green thread at the edges.

Arrange the four long stems and the long leaves over the print piece and press in place.

Prepare the flowers next. Cut out all the petals from brick-colored chintz first (you will need approximately 60 petals) (Fig. 1.18). Cut 7–8 mauve petals for variety.

Cut five backing circles, 1¾″ (4.5cm), from any scrap fabric and arrange approximately 10–12 petals around on top of each circle, adding 1–2 mauve petals to each flower. Use a glue stick to hold them in place on the backing. When finished, cut flower centers from the flowered fabric, or use a fabric of your own choice. Glue that on top of the petals in the center.

Arrange the flowers over the stems and leaves on the wallhanging. Before attaching them, cut out approximately 36 green leaves from green pin-dot fabric (see Fig. 1.18). These are slightly larger, but the same teardrop shape as the flower petals. Slip these leaves behind and around the flowers. Add a

tiny bit of fiberfill behind some of the petals and flower centers to give a trapunto look to the flowers when quilting is completed. Use a glue stick sparingly to hold the leaves and flowers in place.

Now cut out leaves for the top of the vase (Fig. 1.19). Use plain fabrics or those cut from the flowered fabric. (Cut freely, but use this irregular heart shape for all sizes.) Arrange them and glue in place with a glue stick.

Place a leaf and one petal next to the vase on the pin-dot tablecloth as if they've fallen off. Cut out about a dozen tiny ½″ (1.3cm) circles from a yellow/green fabric. Sprinkle those over the stems and leaves.

Cover the picture with black tulle, and pin it in place to hold all the small pieces while stitching.

Prepare the machine for free-quilting by lowering or covering the feed dogs and placing a free-machine, free-quilting, or darning foot on the machine. Use smoke monofilament thread to stitch around the petals and into the flower centers (Fig. 1.20). Stipple the centers (see Fig. 1.8). Continue quilting outside the edges of the leaves and stems (Fig. 1.21); then stitch around the outside of the leaves on top of the vase. Use your imagination as you finish quilting wherever it's needed.

If you find areas that need more batting, slit the backing of the wallhanging and slip fiberfill inside.

1.19 ▪ **The leaves on the vase's top edge are cut in this shape.**

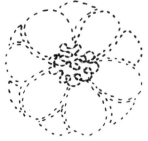

1.20 ▪ **Stitch around the outside of the petals and into the center to stipple the middle area.**

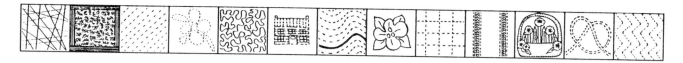

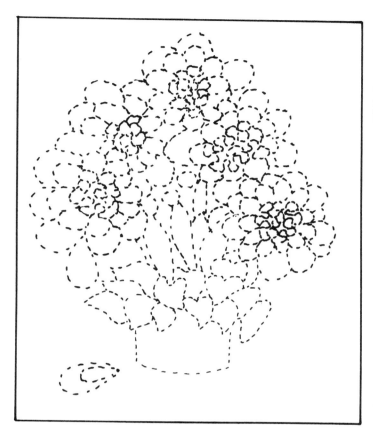

1.21 ▪ **Free-quilt around the outside edges of all the leaves: behind the flowers, at the top of the vase, and between the long leaves and stems.**

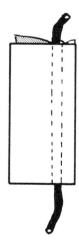

1.22 ▪ **Slip cord between the fabric and batting up to the seam stitches, then trap it there with a row of stitches on the other side.**

Set the machine for regular sewing, and stitch around the outside of the picture to keep the tulle in place.

To make the frame around the collage, cut the striped fabric (1⅓ yd. [1.2m] length) into four lengths, each 5″ (12.5cm) wide. Back the strips with fusible fleece; don't press yet. Stitch ¼″ (6mm) from the edge of the strips, then slip a piece of cording inside the batting against the stitches, and use a zipper foot to stitch on the other side of the cord to hold it in place (Fig. 1.22). Trim batting from the seam allowance. Press the frames to fuse batting in place, but leave 1″ (2.5cm) unpressed along the edges. Now add

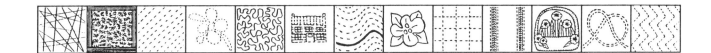

other quilting lines down the length of the strip to hold the fleece and frame together, leaving ¾″ (2cm) open at the edge. Slip cording between batting and fabric, and pull the top fabric around the cord and to the back of the frame (Fig. 1.23). Pin, then use a zipper foot to stitch close to the side of the cable cord.

Next, attach the frame, cut edge nearest center panel. Center and sew on the top and bottom strips first; don't trim back yet. Then pin frames to the sides of the picture, extending them beyond the collage and cutting each side to align with the top and bottom. Go back and stitch the sides to attach them, stopping at the top of the inner edge. Then fold the frame under diagonally on each side, top and bottom, to miter the corners. Baste this by hand, but finish by machine-stitching on the diagonal fold line (Fig. 1.24). Trim.

Place the picture on a flat surface, right side down, and measure for the backing. Then measure the black chintz backing to fit, adding a ½″ (1.3cm) seam allowance all around it. Cut it out, then stitch around the backing on the seam allowance for ease in folding under. Fold under on the stitched lines and press. Place the backing over the picture and pin, then hand-stitch to attach it.

Stitch small plastic rings to the back at each side and center for hanging, or make a casing and hand-stitch it to the top back for a dowel hanger.

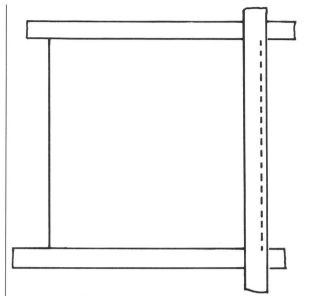

1.23 ▪ **After attaching the border at the top and bottom of your picture, attach the sides. Stitch from top to bottom of the collage, stopping at the inner edge.**

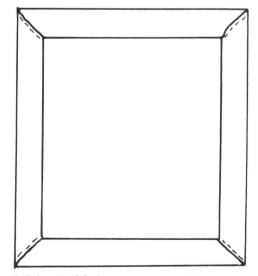

1.24 ▪ **Fold the corners on the diagonal at each corner; baste, then machine-stitch in place.**

YOU WILL NEED:

Fabric: 45″ (1.1m) square flowered chintz

5½″ × 7⅛ yds. (14cm × 6.5m) border print (I found and used instead a wide-stripe fabric for the same effect and needed only a 64″ [1.6m] length of fabric.)

2½ yds. × 45″ (2.3m × 1.1m) black chintz

¾ yd. (68.5cm) black chintz, for welting (optional, for cutting bias 2″ [5cm] wide)

Needle: #90/14 jeans (sharp)

Thread: Smoke-colored monofilament and black sewing; ThreadFuse (optional)

Presser feet: General purpose; free-machine; free-quilting or darning; zipper; walking

Fusible fleece: 2½ yds. × 45″ (2.3m × 1.1m)

Cording: 7 yds. (6.4m) of purchased ½″ (1.3cm) welting, or make your own

Miscellaneous: Quilting pins; silver quilting pencil

1.25 ▪ Use this design to make one tablecloth look like two.

Fool-the-Eye Tablecloth

Here's an idea to fool the eye and pocketbook. Instead of a round, plain black tablecloth covered by a separate flowered square cloth, I combined them into one quilted cloth. The top, a flowered square, is bordered by wide, quilted strips cut from a striped fabric; quilted black chintz is at the bottom of the tablecloth, and that is finished with black covered welting at the bottom edge (Fig. 1.25).

Although these measurements are meant for my table, which is 36″ (.95m) in diameter, with a 20½″ (52cm) drop, you can use

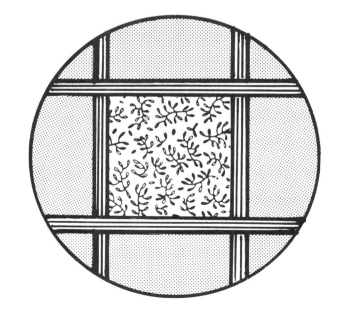

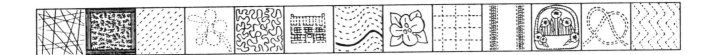

the same construction and quilting ideas for your table, whatever the size. Check out how I figured the measurements for this table; then measure your tabletop and drop length, and begin creating (Fig. 1.26).

Use ¼" (6mm) seam allowances, except for the bottom edge, which is covered with welting and sewn in place with a ½" (1.3cm) seam allowance. For quick construction, use your presser foot edge as a guide if distance from the edge of the foot to the needle is ¼" (6mm). If it isn't, then de-center your needle so the presser foot edge can be a guide for a ¼" (6mm) seam allowance.

First, prepare the striped fabric by cutting 5½" (14cm) strips into four pieces, each 64" (1.63m) long. Stitch down ¼" (6mm) from each side of the strips. (This is the turn-under guide.) Cut fleece to fit within the stitching, place it inside the stitching lines, and fuse to the back. Press under at the stitching.

Cut four pieces of black fabric 17¾" × 45" (45cm × 1.1m) for the sides. Then cut four pieces of the remaining fabric into 11" (27.9cm) squares for the corners.

First pin 11" (28cm) squares to two of the long black pieces of chintz starting at the tops of the short sides (17¾" [45cm]). Then fold in half the short way to find the middle of each. Mark with a silver quilting pencil. Fold the center square also to find the middle of each side. Again, mark with the silver pencil.

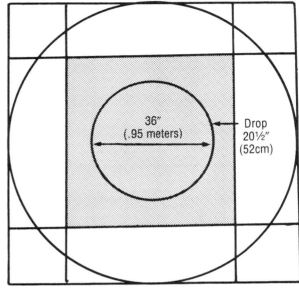

1.26 ▪ **Assemble a square, then cut it into a circle tablecloth.**

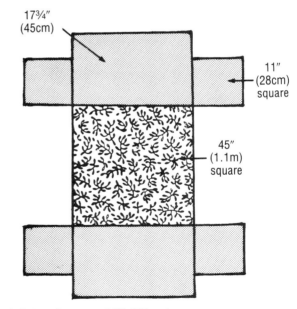

1.27 ▪ **Sew an 11" (28cm) square to each end (short sides) of two black rectangles. Sew these to opposite sides of the center flowered square.**

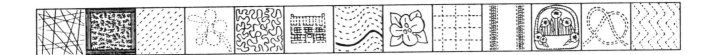

LIVING ROOM **24**

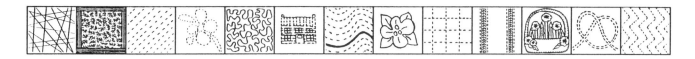

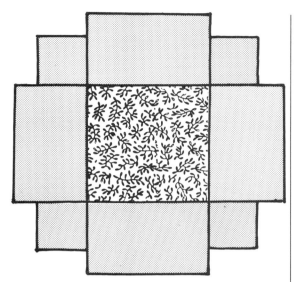

1.28 ▪ **Attach remaining black rectangles to other sides of the flowered square, then to the 11″ (28cm) black squares, as shown.**

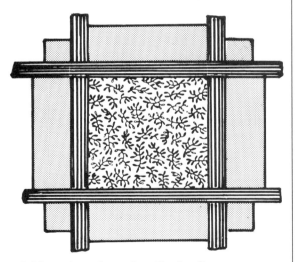

1.29 ▪ **Attach and quilt the four strips.**

With right sides together, match the mark on one side of the flowered square with the mark on one of the black strips. Pin and stitch together.

Repeat centering, pinning, and stitching the opposite side of the flowered square with the other marked black side (Fig. 1.27).

With right sides together, attach one of the remaining black fabric pieces to a side of the flowered square. Stitch the remaining piece of black fabric to the opposite side.

Fold back one long side of the tablecloth at the seam line and pin to the side adjacent to it. Stitch to attach the sides. Continue in the same manner until all sides are sewn together into the tablecloth top (Fig. 1.28). Press seams down.

Appliqué flowered strips at opposite sides of the center square, slightly overlapping the seams so they aren't visible. To do this, stitch on top of the folded edges, using a walking foot. Quilt these strips by straight-stitching down the narrower stripes inside each strip (there are four of them in the strips I used). Then apply the other two strips at the other sides and quilt those, too (Fig. 1.29).

Fold the tablecloth into fourths, measure, and cut the 78″ (1.98m) circle, as shown in Figs. 1.30 and 1.31 (see next page).

Back one section of black chintz with fusible fleece. Press in place and use a few pins to ensure it doesn't shift while sewing. Set up your machine for free-machine quilting by lowering the feed dogs and placing a

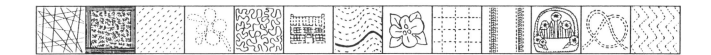

free-machine, free-quilting, or darning foot on the machine, then stipple-quilt the black area with black thread. (Stippling stitches look like the cuts of a jigsaw puzzle; see Fig. 1.8.) After finishing one section, go on to the second, third, and fourth, fusing fleece just before quilting. Quilt the four corners as well.

If you have opted to make your own welting, cover the cord with a strip of bias black fabric 2″ (5cm) wide (see Figs. 4.6–4.11).

Then apply the welting you purchased or made ½″ (1.3cm) from the edge of the cloth. Leave ½″ (1.3cm) free at the start and stitch around the edge, using a zipper foot to nudge the stitches close to the cord. When you come to the end, take the tablecloth off the machine. Butt the cord ends together. Fold under the fabric, overlapping the other side (Fig. 1.32). Place the cloth back under the needle and finish attaching the welting. Stitch the overlap by hand.

When completed, serge or zigzag around the raw edges of the welting and tablecloth. If you use ThreadFuse in the bobbin of your sewing machine, you can then press the edge against the tablecloth and fuse it there. Or turn the welting down and hand-tack the edges in place on back of the tablecloth.

1.30 ▪ **Fold completed pieced tablecloth in half, then quarters.**

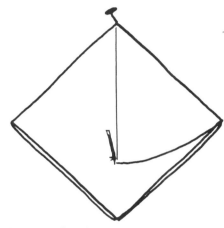

1.31 ▪ **Tack a long piece of string to the folded corner of the tablecloth. Tie a pencil to the other end of the string, then stretch it to reach the radius of the circle and draw a fourth of a circle.**

1.32 ▪ **Attach welting to edge, butting the welting together where it meets. Fold under the fabric at the joining, overlapping the other side. Finish attaching the welting, then stitch the overlap by hand.**

P R O J E C T   3

YOU WILL NEED:

Fabric: 1¼ yds. (1.1m) flowered chintz:

One 16″ (40.5cm) square for backing

One piece 6″ × 30″ (15cm × 76cm)

One strip 6″ × 5⅓ yds. (15cm × 5m)

¾ yd. (68.5cm) black chintz:

One strip 6″ × 24″ (15cm × 61cm)

One strip 5″ × 5⅓ yds. (12.5cm × 4.9m)

Needles: #90/14 universal, hand-sewing

Thread: smoke-colored monofilament; black sewing; black gimp cord, for strengthening buttonholes, or substitute #8 pearl cotton or fine crochet cord.

Presser feet: general purpose; free-machine, free-quilting, or darning; zipper

Fusible fleece (two pieces): one piece 6″ × 16″ (15cm × 40.5cm); one piece 6″ × 12″ (15cm × 30.5cm)

Miscellaneous: 16″ (40.5cm) square pillow form; rotary cutter and mat; 6″ × 24″ (15cm × 61cm) clear plastic ruler; 5⅓ yds. (4.9m) nylon (macrame type) or fine cable cord; silver quilting pencil

1.33 ▪ Assemble the nine-patch as shown.

Nine-Patch Pillow Top

Nine-patch pillows like this are good free-quilting practice pieces. They are small enough to quilt and assemble quickly, and the results are useful and attractive (Fig. 1.33).

Serge or zigzag one edge of the 16″ (40.5cm) flowered backing square (Fig. 1.34). This edge will eventually be turned inside; the treatment keeps it from raveling. Set this aside until later.

Next, fuse fusible fleece to the back of the 6″ × 24″ (15cm × 61cm) piece of black chintz and the 6″ × 30″ (15cm × 76cm) piece of flowered chintz. Then set up the machine for free-quilting by lowering or cover-

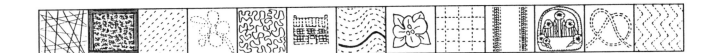

ing the feed dogs and placing a darning foot or free-quilting foot on the machine.

Using black sewing thread, cover the black chintz with the undulating line machine embroiderers call "granite stitch" and quilters call "stippling," which looks like the cut lines on a jigsaw puzzle (see Fig. 1.8, page 16).

The flowered fabric is quilted with smoke monofilament thread by following the flower design: Outline most of the flowers and leaves, sewing into the centers on some and leaving others unquilted (too much quilting will flatten the flowers).

You can move from area to area by raising the presser bar lever and pulling to the next area, without cutting threads. Remember to lower the lever before you stitch again.

Cut the flowered fabric into five 5½" (14cm) squares. Cut the black fabric into four squares the same size as the flowered ones. Then sew the squares into a nine-patch pillow top as shown. (It's not necessary to clip the fusible fleece out of the seam allowance). Stitch a line around the perimeter of the pillow front ¼" (6mm) from the edge.

Next, cut remaining black fabric into 5" (12.5cm) strips, to equal 5⅓ yards (4.9m) long (approximately three times the perimeter of the pillow) on the straight grain. This works fine, but you can cut on the bias if you wish. The straight grain takes less fabric, and you can hide seams in ruffles. Stitch the strips together and join the long strip into a large loop. Fold this the long way for a

1.34 ▪ Serge on one edge of the pillow backing.

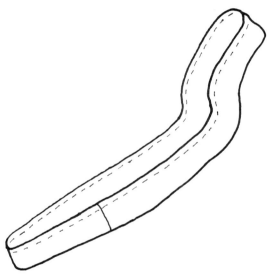

1.35 ▪ Stitch cord inside the fold of the loop.

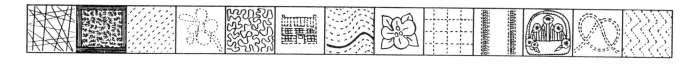

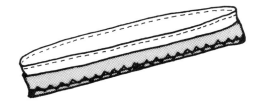

1.36 ▪ **Add a smaller doubled strip, then gather by zigzagging over a cord at the edge.**

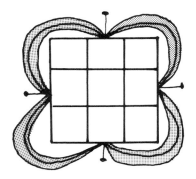

1.37 ▪ **Divide the loop into fourths and pin to pillow edge.**

1.38 ▪ **Pull up the ruffle and stitch to pillow top.**

2½″ (6.5cm) double ruffle and press it.

Follow the same directions for the flowered ruffle, which is cut 6″ (15cm) wide. To make the ruffled edge stand up instead of droop, slip a nylon cord (the size of heavy wrapping twine) into the fold, and using smoke monofilament thread, stitch it in place (Fig. 1.35). Use a zipper foot for this, or use a foot suggested by your machine's manual.

Then construct the ruffle by placing the black fabric over the flowered (cut edges together), folding the strip into four equal parts, and marking the folds with a silver quilting pencil. Unfold.

Use a cording foot and black gimp for gathering. First, place the presser foot at the edge of the two fabrics, then zigzag over the cord all around the edge (Fig. 1.36).

Pin the marks to the center of each of the four sides of the pillow top (cut sides together, corded edge at inside of top) (Fig. 1.37). Pull up on the ruffle, evenly distributing the gathers but allowing more fullness at the corners, and pin; be sure heads of pins are pointing outward (Fig. 1.38). Turn this over and follow the previous stitched line around the nine-patch, removing the pins as you meet them.

Then pin the backing over the ruffles, keeping the ruffles arranged evenly inside. Do this on a flat surface, as the backing is slightly larger than the pillow top. Line up the edges opposite the backing's serged edge and on a side next to it. Pin all four sides. Don't touch the serged side, but trim the

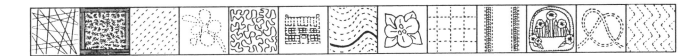

backing back to the seam allowance on the fourth side. (The serged edge will have a wider seam allowance to make stitching the closure easier.)

Don't stitch the serged side yet. From the top, stitch around the other three sides, slightly inside the stitches already there. Then stitch 2″ (5cm) from each corner along the serged side, again inside the stitching line. This leaves an opening for turning. Go back and at each corner stitch 2–3 short, straight stitches diagonally from one side to the next for a better point on the corner (Fig. 1.39). Trim away bulk.

At this point you are ready to turn the pillow case to the outside and insert the pillow form. Before you do that, though, go back and zigzag or serge the three sides to clean up and strengthen them. On the open side, zigzag or serge together the pillow top and backing to the opening at both sides.

Now turn the pillow right side out, pull out the ruffles, and then separate the black and flowered ruffle for a fuller look. Slip in the pillow form and fold under the backing seam allowance at the opening. Invisibly ladder-stitch the pillow opening closed (Fig. 1.40). I like this closure because it makes the pillow look good from both sides.

Hold the pillow at an oblique angle and check for monofilament thread to clip, especially if you jumped from area to area as you stitched. It's hard to see thread ends from straight on.

1.39 ▪ **Stitch backing to pillow top, diagonally stitching the corners, and leaving the top area open for turning.**

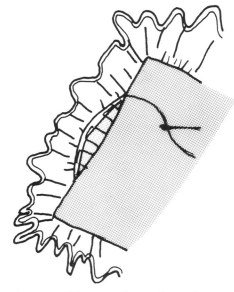

1.40 ▪ **Ladder stitch to close the opening.**

YOU WILL NEED:

Fabric: 18″ × 36″ (46cm × .95m) black chintz

Needles: #80/12; 4mm twin needle; hand-sewing

Thread: 2 spools variegated rayon machine-embroidery (Sulky #942), or wind a bobbin for the second spool; black sewing

Presser feet: Edge-stitch, blind-hem, or open embroidery; general purpose; zipper

Fusible fleece: 18″ × 36″ (46cm × .95m)

Bias tape (single-fold): One 4-yd. (3.7m) card each: mauve, light yellow, dark yellow, light blue, peach, ivory, light green, deep rose

Piping: 2 yds. (1.85m) black, purchased or made

Miscellaneous: 16″ (40.5cm) pillow form; silver quilting pencil; chalk; yardstick

Reversible Pillow Top

This is a reversible quilted pillow with strips of bias tape sewn on one side of the pillow and twin-needle quilting on the other side (Fig. 1.41). The bias tape fringe works for both sides. To make it reversible, I closed the opening at one edge with hand-stitching.

Cut the black fabric into two 18″ (46cm) squares. Prepare one square by drawing lines horizontally, vertically, and diagonally

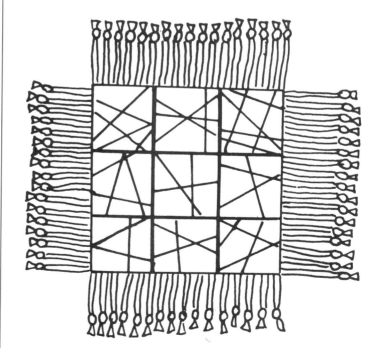

1.41 ▪ Use bias tape to decorate a reversible pillow.

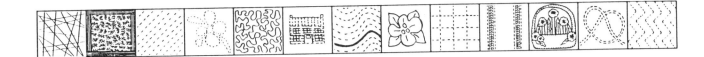

over it with the quilting pencil and yardstick (Fig. 1.42). Don't be shy; you'll need many lines, and placement isn't supposed to be studied. The only caution is to keep the lines apart; in other words, to eliminate bulk, don't have too many lines intersecting at the same place.

Back the square with fusible fleece and attach the bias tape, using the drawn lines as guides. To do this, place the edge of each piece of bias slightly over a pencil line to cover it, so you won't have to sponge out the pencil line later (Fig. 1.43). Use variegated rayon machine-embroidery thread and a decorative stitch on your machine when stitching the bias in place. (I used the blanket stitch, but you can get almost the same effect with a blind-hem stitch.) Don't cut the bias first, but apply a strip, cut, then go on to another and another.

It's not necessary to pin the bias in place. Choose colors at random. First stitch on a vertical line, then a horizontal one, then another that crosses one or both of the others. Continue crossing and recrossing bias strips. Careful, don't stretch the bias while stitching.

Next, cut the bias tape pillow top into nine squares, each 5¾"(14.5cm) square. Once cut, the fun begins. Arrange and rearrange them so you're pleased with the layout. If you want to add a few cheater pieces of bias to fill out a square, do so. (I won't tell.)

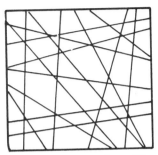

1.42 ▪ Draw lines on the pillow top for bias placement.

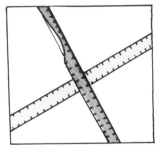

1.43 ▪ Use a decorative stitch at each side of the bias tape to attach it, being sure to cover pencil lines.

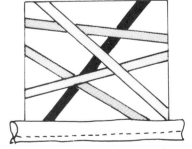

1.44 ▪ Attach piping to the edge of a square.

Fool-the-Eye Tablecloth (Project 2),
Yo-yo Basket Pillow (Project 5),
and Petticoat Lampshade Cover
(Project 6).

Opposite: Machine-Quilted Sampler, showcasing stitches and techniques (Project 1). *This page, above:* Reversible Pillow Top (Project 4), featuring bias-decorated side, and Nine-Patch Pillow Top (Project 3). *Below:* Reversible Pillow Top, showing the side with twin-needle quilting.

Scraps and Sheers Shower Curtain traps cotton fabric scraps between layers of sparkle organza and cotton (Project 8). *Opposite, top:* Two-Towel Bath Mat (Project 9); *below:* 3-D Appliqué Guest Towel (Project 12), Ribbons and Decorative Stitches Guest Towel (Project 11), Appliquéd and Embroidered Guest Towel (Project 10).

Summer Quilt of buffalo-check flannel (Project 14), and Ribbonwork Felt Wallhanging which may also be made as a table runner (Project 18). *Opposite, top:* Leather Indian Basket (Project 17); *below:* Leather Patch and Piece Pillow (Project 15); and Leather Ribbon Pillow (Project 16).

Penny-Rug Wallhanging (Project 7). Traditionally made of tightly woven woolens, this penny rug utilizes today's heavy, colorful, easy-finish felts.

Sea and Shells Collage makes a charming addition to the bath—or any room you choose (Project 13).

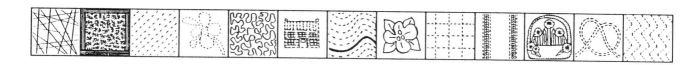

Construct the pillow top in three columns: Change to black sewing thread and stitch piping to the bottom edge of the square in the upper left-hand corner (Fig. 1.44). Use a zipper foot, or whatever your machine manual suggests, to get close to the piping. Then seam the middle left square to the first one. Open the squares. Stitch piping to the bottom edge of the second square and add the third square in that row. Go on to the middle three squares and add piping to the squares as you did previously. Continue until you have three strips of squares.

Go back and stitch the strips together, with piping between (Fig. 1.45). Your nine patches are now a pillow top. Straight-stitch around the perimeter, ¼″ (6mm) from the edge. Set this aside till later.

Find the other black square of fabric. Back it with fusible fleece, then draw horizontal, vertical, and diagonal lines with chalk and a yardstick.

Use a 4mm twin needle and the same variegated rayon thread used on the front. Straddle the chalk lines to mimic the bias-tape appliquéd front (Fig. 1.46).

Before you sew the pillow together, use the leftover bias pieces to make a fringe around the edge (you'll need approximately 6 yds. [5.5m] of bias for the fringe). Cut it all into 6″ (15cm) lengths and stitch the fringe to the edge by placing two pieces

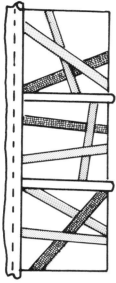

1.45 ▪ After stitching three squares together, add piping along the side.

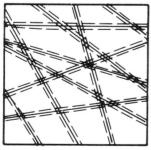

1.46 ▪ Use a twin needle to stitch on either side of your drawn line.

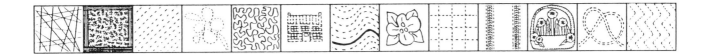

(wrong sides) together and stitching them to the front (Fig. 1.47).

Before you assemble the pillow, trim the back to 16″ (40.5cm) square. Then place the pillow front on a flat surface and cover it with the back, right sides together. Check to see that the bias fringe won't get caught when stitching the edge. Pin in place. Take the pillow case to your machine and stitch from the front side, slightly inside the line of stitches already there. Complete stitching three sides. On the fourth side, stitch in 2″ (5cm) from each corner. Then go back and stitch 2–3 short, straight stitches diagonally at each corner and trim bulk from them (see Fig. 1.39). To strengthen, serge or zigzag all the edges except the opening.

Turn the pillowcase to the right side and insert the pillow form. If you feel the corners need more filling, use a handful of fiberfill in each. Stitch the opening together invisibly by hand.

Knot the ends of each set of bias fringe (Fig. 1.48). Lengths may vary a bit and knots may not be exactly the same distance from the pillow, so trim if you wish, but exactness is not next to godliness.

1.47 ▪ **Attach strips of bias tape to pillow edges to create fringe.**

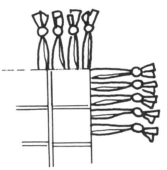

1.48 ▪ **Turn pillow to outside and knot bias tape at the ends.**

P R O J E C T 5

Fabric: 16″ (41cm) square flowered chintz, for the front

17″ (43cm) square flowered chintz, for the back

16″ (41cm) square blue-and-white checked chintz

Two pieces each light and dark green chintz 15″ × 10″ (38cm × 25.5cm), for leaves and stems

Six scraps of compatible fabrics, for yo-yos

16″ × 32″ (40.5cm × 81.5cm) muslin, for pillow form

Needle: #80/12 universal

Thread: Clear monofilament; green and black sewing

Presser feet: General purpose; shirring (optional)

Miscellaneous: Two 16″ (40.5cm) squares fusible interfacing; 2 yds. (1.8m) red pearl cotton; bag of fiberfill; 12″ (30.5cm) Velcro strip

Yo-yo Basket Pillow

I keep telling everyone that I have to simplify my life, and eliminating the pillow clutter on the couch would be an excellent start. I've also been known to groan at anything resembling a yo-yo. So what do I do but make another pillow by combining a half-dozen printed fabrics (now I have *pattern* clutter, too) and fill it with yo-yos! I like it.

Buying pillows is easy, but unless you want to spend a fortune for custom-made creations, your choices are limited.

1.49 ▪ **Design for the yo-yo pillow.**

I like making my own pillows because I can use removable pillow forms. Buy a pillow today and you probably won't get a removable case. If you wash the pillow, the entire pillow has to be tossed into the washing machine and the results are usually less than acceptable.

Making a pillow form is sometimes a must because of a pillow's size and shape. For this odd-shaped pillow, I made the form by cutting out two 16″ (41cm) squares of muslin, rounding off the top two corners, then zigzag-stitching around all but the bottom edge. After filling the form firmly with fiberfill, I closed the bottom with zigzag stitches. Of course, you can use your serger if you have one.

To make the yo-yo pillow top, I chose the same fabrics I used for the other accessories in the room (Fig. 1.49).

First, back the smaller square of flowered chintz and the blue-and-white checked fabric with iron-on interfacing to stiffen them. Cut the front basket fabric into the shape shown (Fig. 1.50).

Stitch around the opening of the basket and cut out the center, leaving ¼″ (6mm) seam allowance (Fig. 1.51). Clip to the stitching around the curve and into the corners. Fold under all around inside the opening and use a glue stick to keep seam allowance in place. Place on top of the checked fabric and pin at top, bottom, and side edges.

Cut out the yo-yos; five large circles are 6″

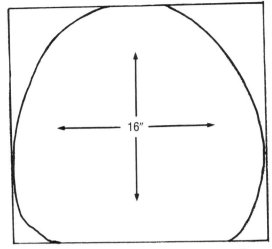

1.50 ▪ Cut out 16″ (41cm) square of muslin, then cut into pillow's rounded basket shape.

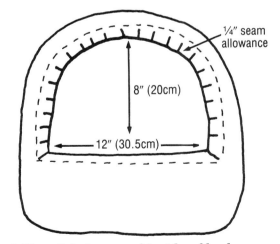

1.51 ▪ Stitch around inside of basket and clip the curved edge.

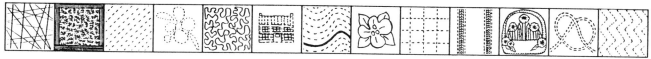

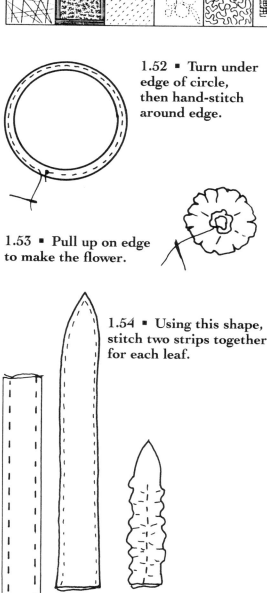

1.52 ▪ Turn under edge of circle, then hand-stitch around edge.

1.53 ▪ Pull up on edge to make the flower.

1.54 ▪ Using this shape, stitch two strips together for each leaf.

1.55 ▪ Gather centers of leaves.

1.56 ▪ Stitch two 15″ (38cm) strips together into a tube.

(15cm) in diameter, and one smaller circle is 4″ (10cm) in diameter. Turn under the edge ⅛″ (3mm) and sew a running stitch by hand around the yo-yos. Pull up into a circle to make the yo-yo flower (Figs. 1.52 and 1.53).

To make the leaves, cut out two 10″ (25.5cm) long strips of light and dark green fabric, 1½″ (4cm) wide. With right sides together, stitch into leaf shapes, leaving bottoms open (Fig. 1.54), then trim, turn, and press. Gather up the center, using the shirring foot on your machine, or stitch down the centers by hand and pull up to gather (Fig. 1.55). Then make four more leaves 6″ (15cm) long. Cut two of the leaf strips 1½″ (4cm) wide (for leaves inside the basket), and two more 1¼″ (3cm) wide (to slip under the yo-yos on top of the basket).

Cut out one light green stem strip 1¼″ × 15″ (3cm × 38cm). Cut one the same size from the dark green fabric. With right sides together, stitch the two together at the sides (Fig. 1.56) and turn right side out.

Cut off two stems, each 4″ (10cm) long, leaving a 7″ (18cm) stem for the center of the basket (Fig. 1.57, page 38).

Arrange the flowers, stems, and leaves as shown on the next page in Fig. 1.58 (slip the stems and leaves under the basket, light green on top), and pin all of them in place. Remove the basket and apply the stems with green thread and a blanket stitch at the edges. Then stitch the centers of the leaves with a straight stitch of clear monofilament

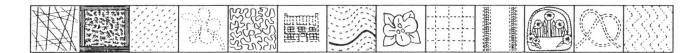

thread. Use the same thread to tack down the centers of the yo-yos to hold them in place over the stems.

Put the basket back in place and blanket-stitch around the opening with black thread. Stitch around the outside of the basket with the same stitch, 1/4″ (6mm) from the pillow-top edge (Fig. 1.59).

Add the leaves and yo-yos to each corner of the basket and stitch them in the same way you applied the others (Fig. 1.60). Wind pearl cotton around your fingers 10 times and tie in the center. Use monofilament to zigzag on top of the ties in the center of each yo-yo for fringed centers (Figs. 1.61 and 1.62). Clip loops and trim. Flatten, then hand-tack around the yo-yos to hold the edges down.

Prepare the back piece by using Velcro for the opening. Cut the backing in half vertically. Turn one side under 1″ (2.5cm); turn the other side over 1″ (2.5cm) (Fig. 1.63). On both sides, stitch around Velcro to attach. Press Velcro together and pin the folded edges together at both sides. Stitch on top of the fold above and below the Velcro, then make another line of stitching on top of the cut edges above and below the Velcro to hold the backing together (Fig. 1.64).

Place front and back right sides together and stitch around the basket at the edge, making 1/4″ (6mm) seam allowance. Trim the backing to match the pillow front. Either

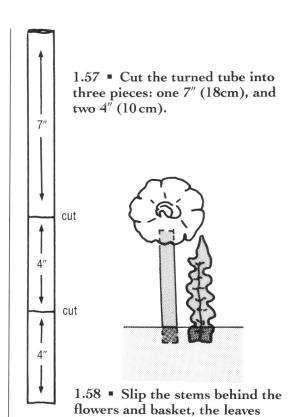

1.57 ▪ **Cut the turned tube into three pieces: one 7″ (18cm), and two 4″ (10cm).**

1.58 ▪ **Slip the stems behind the flowers and basket, the leaves behind the basket.**

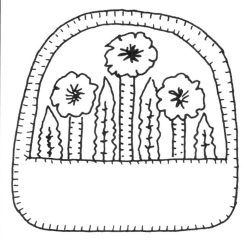

1.59 ▪ **Blanket-stitch around the outside and inside of the basket as shown.**

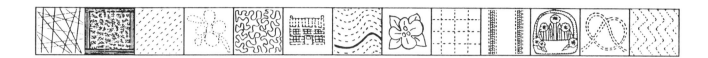

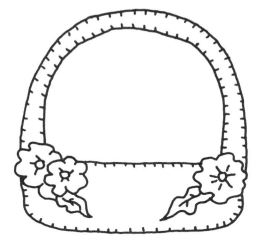

1.60 • Place a large and small yo-yo at one corner, a large yo-yo at the other. Attach a gathered leaf at each side.

1.61 • Wrap pearl cotton around your fingers and tie in the center.

1.62 • Stitch pearl cotton in the center of the yo-yo.

zigzag or serge around the edges. Turn right side out.

Slip in the pillow form you've made and close the back. Remember to add extra fiber-fill if needed to fill out the shape.

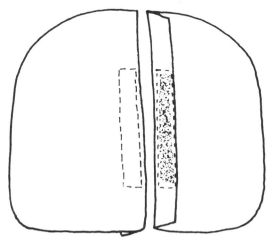

1.63 • Turn under the edge of one side, turn over the other side; attach Velcro strips to both sides.

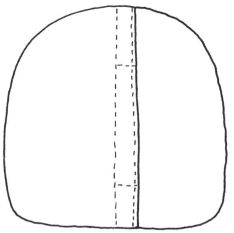

1.64 • Stitch two sides together above and below the Velcro.

Petticoat Lampshade Cover

This is an ancient idea for covering a small lampshade. My mother didn't invent them, but she made them so often through the years that her name should go on them instead of the real one: petticoat cover (Fig. 1.65). She showed me how and now I make them, too, because they are easy, super-fast, and a pattern isn't needed. I've revamped the construction, now that I'm a serger person, but using a sewing machine is fine. When I mention a serger in the directions, you can use your sewing machine to seam and use zigzag or serpentine (multiple zigzag) stitches to finish the edges.

First measure the plain shade on your lamp. You'll need to know the circumference of it at the top, the bottom, and the height of the shade measured along the slant of the shade (Fig. 1.66). (I like these covers best on shades that are narrower at the top than at the bottom.)

Let's use my small shade as an example (Fig. 1.67): At the top the circumference is 21″ (53.5cm), at the bottom it's 34″ (86.5cm). The shade is 9″ (23cm) along the slant. With these measurements you can cut the fabrics for the shade cover and lining, both the same size.

YOU WILL NEED:
Fabric: Top and lining (see above)
Needle: #80/12 universal
Thread: Matching sewing
Presser feet: General purpose; buttonhole
Miscellaneous: Vanishing marker; yardstick; ⅜″ (9.5mm) grosgrain ribbon to match (length = circumference of upper lampshade + 36″ [.95m]); 1″ × ½″ (2.5cm × 1.3cm) iron-on interfacing; Stop Fraying

1.65 ▪ **Petticoat Lampshade Cover.**

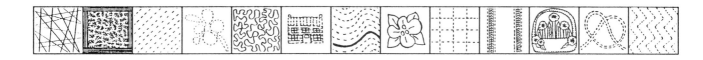

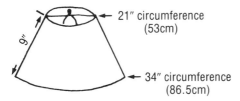

21" circumference
(53cm)

9"

34" circumference
(86.5cm)

1.66 ▪ Take measurements of the
circumference at top and bottom, and
the height of the lampshade to make
your own lampshade cover.

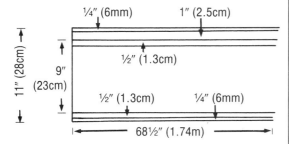

¼" (6mm) 1" (2.5cm)

½" (1.3cm)

11" (28cm)

9"
(23cm)

½" (1.3cm) ¼" (6mm)

68½" (1.74m)

1.67 ▪ Measurements for my
lampshade cover.

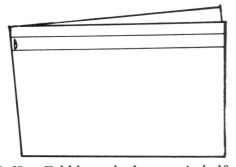

1.68 ▪ Fold lampshade cover in half
to find buttonhole placement.

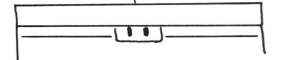

1.69 ▪ Back buttonhole placement
with fusible interfacing.

There is a 1″ (2.5cm) ruffle at the top, under that a ½″ (1.3cm) casing for ribbon, 9″ (23cm) for the shade, and ½″ (1.3cm) overhang. Therefore, the length of the fabric is 1″ + 9″ (2.5cm + 23cm) + ½″ (1.3cm) overhang; add ½″ (1.3cm) for two ¼″ (6mm) seam allowances, for a total of 11″ (28cm). Width is predicated on the circumference at the lower edge, 34″ (86.5cm), which is doubled; 68″ (1.65m) + ½″ (1.3cm) for seam allowances = 68½″ (1.75m).

Cut out both pieces of fabric, for shade cover and lining, 11″ × 68½″ (28cm × 1.75m). If you must piece fabric, it won't be noticeable because seams are lost in the gathers and don't show.

Prepare the front of the lampshade by drawing stitching lines 1¼″ (3cm) from the top edge of your fabric and ½″ (1.3cm) down from the first line to create the ribbon casing. To find the center and place the buttonholes, place the cut edges of the shade cover together and fold the fabric in half the short way (Fig. 1.68). Mark two lines for vertical buttonholes in the ribbon casing area, one on either side of the fold, leaving about ¼″ (6mm) between buttonholes. Iron on a scrap of fusible interfacing behind the buttonhole marks (Fig. 1.69), then use your sewing machine with thread to match the lampshade fabric to make buttonholes. Open the buttonholes.

Next, place the top sides of the front and

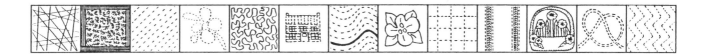

lining fabrics together and serge both long edges, using ¼" (6mm) seams (Fig. 1.70). Turn the tube to the right side and press top and bottom seams.

Take the lampshade back to your sewing machine and straight-stitch both marked casing lines (Fig. 1.71).

The length of the ⅜" (9.5cm) grosgrain ribbon is estimated by using the top lampshade measurement (21" [53.5cm]) and adding 36" (.95m) for the bow. First, cut the ribbon in half. Thread one piece through the casing from the cut edge of the lampshade cover through the buttonhole. Repeat on the other side. Pull out just a bit beyond the edge and pin (Fig. 1.72). Place right sides of the tube together, pin, and serge the edges together.

Turn the lampshade cover to the right side. Pull up on the ribbon and gather the top to fit your lampshade. Tie the ribbon into a bow. Trim the ribbon ends to the length you wish and use Stop Fraying at the edges. Now, what could be more simple? I think I'll make another one!

VARIATIONS:

1. Use organdy and hem-stitches. (Scallop the edges for a great look, or use an edge-scalloped embroidered fabric.)

2. Run a ribbon or elastic casing at the top and bottom (this works especially well with a lampshade that is the same width at the top and bottom).

1.70 ▪ Machine-stitch or serge the lining and lampshade fabric together on the long edges.

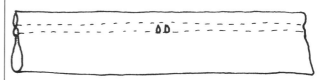

1.71 ▪ Stitch in a ribbon casing.

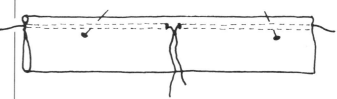

1.72 ▪ Thread ribbon through both sides before serging the lampshade cover into a circle.

P R O J E C T   7

Fabric: Two pieces of black felt, each 30″ × 48″ (76cm × 1.2m); colored felt, scraps or ¼ yd. (23cm) each, in mauve, yellow, blue, green, ivory, rose, pink

Needle: #80/12 universal

Thread: Black sewing

Presser foot: Open-embroidery or cording

Cord: 22 yards (20.1m) black velverette or chenille yarn; black cord for hanging

Miscellaneous: Rotary cutter and mat; yardstick; plastic template material; tacky glue; chalk; dowel

Penny Rug Wallhanging

Once penny rugs were made with circles, using coins, spools, and buttons as patterns. This wallhanging uses 3″ (7.5cm), 2″ (5cm), and 1″ (2.5 cm) templates cut from heavy plastic. Although you can make the wallhanging any size, you will need 104 circles of each size for this one (Fig. 1.73).

As a color guide, match the flowered fabric in this room decor.

Penny rugs were traditionally made with tightly woven woolen pieces, but I opted for felt because today there are so many felt

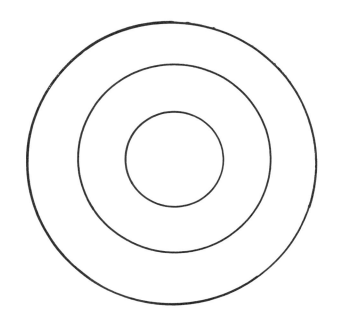

1.73 ▪ **Use these three circles as patterns for your penny rug wallhanging.**

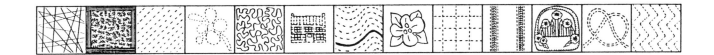

choices: It comes in many grades, widths, and beautiful colors. The edges don't have to be finished, so it is an excellent choice for this project. Although most stores offer more than one weight of felt, I always buy the heaviest weight.

To make the hanging, draw a chalk grid on one piece of black felt, starting with the first vertical line 4½″ (11.5cm) from the left edge. Draw eight vertical lines, 3″ (7.6cm) apart.

Begin drawing the horizontal lines, starting 6″ (15cm) from the top. Draw 13 horizontal lines, 3″ (7.6cm) apart (Fig. 1.74).

You will need 104 felt circles of each size. Cut 14–15 of each color in each size. After cutting out all the circles, arrange them in stacks of three each on the backing, rearranging the colors until you are pleased. Then dab the back of the top two circles with tacky glue and return the stacks to the black background. Pin in place, putting the center of the circles at intersections of lines. (Yes, the circles will touch.)

Lay black velverette or chenille yarn (it looks like felt when stitched in place) over the grid lines and circles. Using black thread, couch over the yarn with a zigzag (stitch width 3; stitch length 2), using a cording or open-embroidery foot (Fig. 1.75). Then zigzag-stitch across the horizontal lines, intersecting the black cords in the centers of the circles.

Leave 1″ (2.5cm) at each end of the yarn.

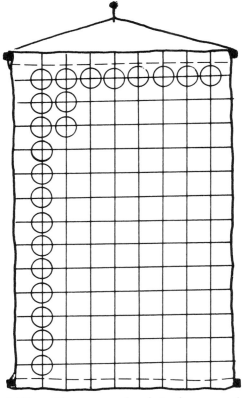

1.74 ▪ **Place a stack of circles at each grid intersection.**

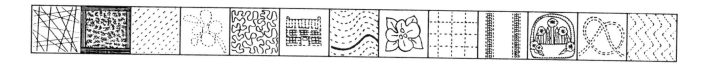

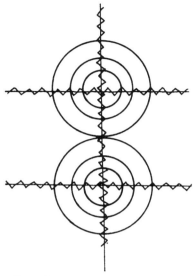

1.75 ▪ **Couch yarn over the circles with a zigzag stitch.**

Fold it back underneath the black felt and catch it as you stitch on top.

To apply the lining, place the right sides of the lining and finished top together and stitch ½" (1.3cm) from the edges. Turn the wallhanging right side out and press the stitched edges. Finish by folding under the top casing 1" (2.5cm) and stitching across the cut edge. Fold under the bottom hem 1" (2.5cm) and straight-stitch in place as you did the top. Slip dowels into the top and bottom casings. Tack the hanging cord at each end of the top dowel.

VARIATION:

Omit casings and use your wallhanging as a table cover or trunk throw, which was the style in the Gay Nineties when penny rugs were the rage.

CHAPTER 2

Bathroom

"Why make your own shower curtain?" a friend asked. Why, indeed. First—and last—of all, this shower curtain is going to be the focal point of an otherwise boring bathroom. Once completed, I can go on from there to decorate with more enthusiasm. One small decoration I added is a collage of sheers and overlays. Then, during a visit to a linen outlet, I found the towels I needed to make a bath mat. With a design already printed on one towel, I easily followed the lines of the motifs to quickly quilt a rug. I purchased other towels I could decorate for guests. The bathroom is developing a personality!

The projects for this bathroom are: Scraps and Sheers Shower Curtain, Two-Towel Bath Mat, Appliquéd and Embroidered Guest Towel, Ribbons and Decorative Stitches Guest Towel, 3-D Appliqué Guest Towel, Sea and Shells Collage.

P R O J E C T   8

YOU WILL NEED:

Fabric: 4½ yds. × 38½″ (4.2m × 98cm), for the underlayer of the curtain (I used blue polished cotton); 4⅝ yds. × 38½″ (4.2m × 98cm) transparent fabric for the top layer (I used polyester sparkle organza); scraps or ¼ yd. (23cm) each of seven colors of cotton (see text for the colors I used)

Needle: #80/12

Thread: Blue cotton sewing thread; rayon variegated machine-embroidery (Sulky #942)

Presser feet: General purpose; free-machine, darning foot or spring, or free-quilting

Fusibles: 2 yds. (1.85m) of 1″ (2.5cm) paper-backed Lite HeatnBond; 4½ yds. × 1 yd. (4.2m × .95m) paper-backed fusible web (e.g., Pellon's Wonder Under); 2 yds. (1.85m) belt interfacing (e.g., Pellon's Waist Shaper)

Miscellaneous: Rotary cutter and mat; 6″ × 24″ (15cm × 61cm) clear plastic ruler; plastic shower liner with hooks; two rubber fingers from an office-supply store (optional)

2.1 ▪ **Measure and cut two pieces of cotton and two pieces of sparkle organza as shown.**

Scraps and Sheers Shower Curtain

Once I was in a home dec frame of mind, I could imagine the following technique also for tablecloths, pillows, and valences. Depending on fabrics chosen and how they're stitched together, there is no limit to uses for the new fabric you can create.

The standard measurement for a shower curtain is: 72″ × 72″ (1.85m × 1.85m). Double-check for your shower by measuring from the top under the rod to the desired length. You need more fabric for hems and edges, so add 3″ (7.5cm) for upper and 2″ (5cm) for lower hems (Fig. 2.1). Add 2″

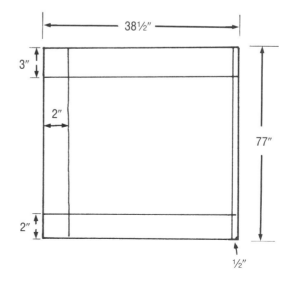

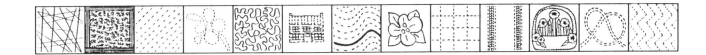

(5cm) to each side. This curtain is constructed in two parts that are sewn together. Hang it from the rod in front of a clear plastic liner.

Begin by cutting up the scraps of cotton colors you want in the curtain. I used these: light and dark peach, yellow, light and dark green, dark blue, lavender. Use the rotary cutter to cut it all into 1″ (2.5cm) strips, then layer the strips on top of each other and cut them into tiny shreds. Place the colored shreds into a large box, mix them up, and put them aside.

Cut the blue polished cotton and organza in halves, the short way. Next, press the fusible web to the top side of the polished cotton and remove the paper. Still working on the ironing board, line up the organza to the side and top of the fused cotton. Pin, then press across the top edge with a wool setting to hold layers together.

Lift up the top layer and scatter mixed shreds of colored fabric over the bottom layer. Replace the top layer and press. Use a wool setting and a dry iron to press each place for three seconds across the curtain to fuse the layers and trap the fabric scraps. (It is not necessary to use a press cloth if you follow these directions.)

Move the fabrics down, scatter scraps under the top layer and press again. Continue till you get to the bottom of the curtain. Turn the curtain over and press from the back side, too. No, the fusible web doesn't

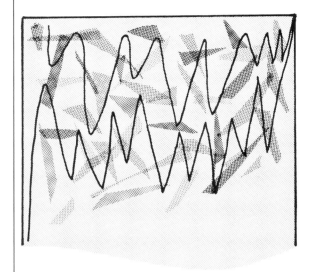

2.2 ▪ **Trap fabric scraps between cotton and organza and zigzag-stitch over the sandwich.**

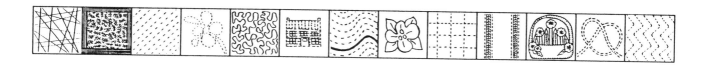

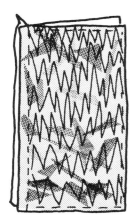

2.3 ▪ **Seam wrong sides together.**

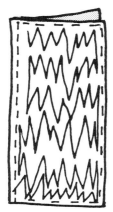

2.4 ▪ **Turn and seam again to hide raw edges (French seam).**

show. And it doesn't gum up the iron, because the iron is never so hot that it causes the web to melt through the organza. Complete the other half as you did the first.

Before you begin to stitch the fused layers, fill at least six bobbins with a sewing thread color that matches the backing fabric. Use cotton thread to help prevent stretching. (Polyester stretches slightly.)

On top, use rayon variegated machine-embroidery thread (Sulky #942). Set up your machine for free-machining by lowering or covering the feed dogs and using a free-quilting foot on your machine. (You could use the general-purpose foot and the reverse button on your machine for the following, but it would take a much longer time.)

Begin at the top left, and stitch up and down in long, uneven zigzags across the top (approximately 4" [10cm] long) (Fig. 2.2). No need to stitch fast, but move the curtain slowly and stitch at a moderate speed. Look at your stitches. If they are too long (you control this by the speed you move the fabric), move the curtain more slowly or sew at a faster speed. When you reach the other side, start back again, stitching about 4" (10cm) lower and then up and down in zigzags across the curtain. Continue in this manner and work your way across and to the bottom of the curtain.

Here's a helpful hint: The organza is so slippery, and manipulating it so frustrating, that you need help. I bought two "rubber fin-

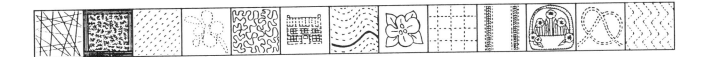

gers" for my index fingers. (Buy them at office-supply stores. They come in sizes, like thimbles.) Or cut tips off balloons, if you have them, and slip them on your fingers. You may also find a square of grid-like rubber in your kitchen. It's meant for protecting wood finishes from metal lamps and for opening jars. Now it's also meant for moving organza easily. Cut the square in half so you can place your fingertips on it. Any of these ideas makes sewing organza a breeze.

When your stitching is finished, stitch around both sections a presser foot's width away from the edge, and then clean up all the edges by cutting off any scraps or frayed edges.

Place wrong sides of the long edges together and pin. Stitch with blue sewing thread from top to bottom with the side of the presser foot on top of the cut edges (this is the curtain's center seam). Trim the seam (Fig. 2.3, page 49). Turn the curtain, right sides together, and press on the seam. Pin and stitch from top to bottom, with presser foot edge on the fold, enclosing the raw edges (Fig. 2.4, page 49). Press the seam to one side.

Then press the fusible strips to the under-sides of both side edges. Fold under and press to fuse (Fig. 2.5). Fold again and pin. Change thread to variegated rayon again, and stitch at the edge of the curtain from the top. Then, from the top side, stitch again on the fold. Attach a seam guide to your

2.5 ▪ **Fuse webbing strip to sides, fold under twice, and stitch down both folds.**

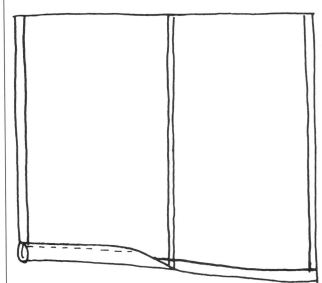

2.6 ▪ **Fuse, then fold up the bottom edge and stitch at the top fold.**

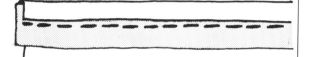

2.7 ▪ **Place fusible belt stiffener (Pellon's Waist Shaper) at the top, perforations 3″ (7.6cm) from the top edge of the curtain.**

2.8 ▪ **Fold top edge under to perforations.**

2.9 ▪ **Fold over again at the perforations and stitch in place.**

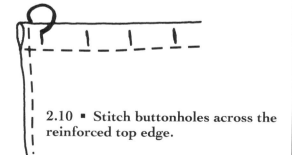

2.10 ▪ **Stitch buttonholes across the reinforced top edge.**

machine, or place a strip of tape on the machine bed so you can measure and stitch a straight line exactly on top of that fold, which isn't visible from the top.

Follow the same procedure for the bottom hem, but first press on a 1″ (2.5cm) fusible strip. Fold up on this line and press. Fold up again, pin, and stitch on the fold (Fig. 2.6).

The top double hem is 1½″ (3.8cm) deep. Press down 3″ (7.6cm) from the top, then open. Place belt fusible across the fold (narrow edge at top) and match the fold perforations with the fold line you've pressed (Fig. 2.7). Press the fusible in place. Fold the shower curtain under at top to meet the interfacing fold. Fold at the perforations, press, and pin. Stitch across the bottom fold (Figs. 2.8 and 2.9).

Use the shower liner as a guide for buttonhole placement. Change to blue cotton sewing thread to stitch ¾″ (2cm) vertical buttonholes, ½″ (1.3cm) from the top of the curtain. Cut them open. Slip shower curtain rings into the liner and curtain (Fig. 2.10) and hang it on the shower rod.

I love the sheer organza look so I'll use it for the small undersea collage later in this chapter.

VARIATIONS:

1. Use organzas on top and underneath for a curtain.

2. Try transparent scraps between two pieces of organza.

P R O J E C T   9

Two-Towel Bath Mat

Make a quick, quilted bath mat that not only feels great on the toes, but also matches your towels—because it's made from your towels.

Look for a large towel with a design to quilt. This one matches the bathroom color scheme: brick red, blue, mauve, green, yellow, off-white, and black. Buy other towels like it to use as towels.

The bath towel for the back is slightly larger than the printed towel, exactly what's needed. Towels usually have a decorative strip about 6″ (15cm) from each edge. Those decorative strips often scrunch up when laundered, so be safe and cut them off (Fig. 2.11). And sometimes the design on a printed towel isn't centered, as was the case with this one, so before you begin to quilt, use a rotary cutter, mat, and ruler to even up the design and trim both towels where needed. Then place one on top of the other and trim to the same size.

Fuse the fleece to the underside of the top towel (Fig. 2.12). Baste around the edges (optional). Next, place the top side of the printed towel on the top side of the other towel, line up the edges, and pin the towel

YOU WILL NEED:

Two towels: One decorative for the top, the other that coordinates with the top towel and is slightly larger

Fusible fleece: 25″ × 45″ (64cm × 1.1m)

Needle: #90/14 jeans (sharp)

Thread: Polyester sewing, to match backing; clear nylon monofilament

Presser foot: Walking or general purpose

Miscellaneous: Rotary cutter and mat; 6″ × 24″ (15cm × 61cm) clear plastic ruler; yardstick

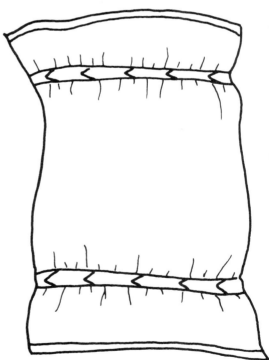

2.11 ▪ **Cut off up to and including the decorative strips at top and bottom.**

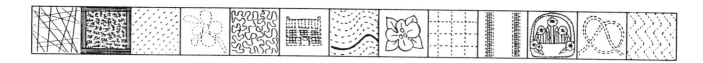

2.12 ▪ Baste fusible fleece to the underside of the decorative towel.

2.13 ▪ Stitch towels together, front to front. Round corners and leave an area unstitched for turning.

sandwich together. Beginning at the middle of one side, stitch around the towels, ending about 12″ (30.5cm) from the starting point. (You'll turn the rug right side out at this opening.) Trim back the batting to the stitching line, then go back to the corners and round them off (Fig. 2.13). Cut away the bulk at the corners so they lie flat when the towels are turned right side out.

To flatten them, zigzag the edges (stitch width 3; stitch length 1). If you have a serger, serge the edges instead.

Pull the towels through the opening so the right side is now on the outside. Push out the corners carefully with a blunt tool. (I have a stuffing tool made from a dowel that is perfect for the job; see Chapter 4, "Quilting/ Sewing Shortcuts.") Take the rug to your ironing board and, from the outside, press the seams to flatten them. Hand-stitch the opening closed.

Place the rug on a table or floor and smooth it flat. Look at the top towel. If you haven't planned the lines of quilting yet, do so now.

Pin the layers together if needed, or merely smooth out the layers and roll up the mat.

If you have a walking foot, use it, or use the general-purpose foot. Change your top thread to clear monofilament. For the bobbin use a polyester thread the same color as the bottom towel. Begin and end each line of stitching by either stitching up and back a

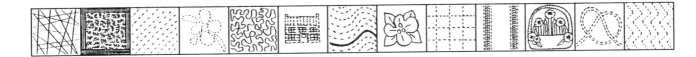

couple of stitches, or stitching in one place by lifting up the presser foot lever to keep the fabric in place as you anchor the stitches.

The rug is small and manipulating it isn't difficult. If there are any straight, long lines, stitch them in first (Fig. 2.14). This holds the layers together and you can get rid of any basting pins you used. Then sew the straight passes from one side of the mat to the other.

This towel has a multi-colored Persian rug design on it (Fig. 2.15). It's easy to follow the design, traveling from one motif to another so there aren't too many starts and stops. Quilt lines close enough so they are at least within a hand's width, yet not so close that the puffy, quilted look is lost.

The mat is reversible. For a towel bath mat variation, see my book, *Twenty Easy Machine-Made Rugs.*

2.14 ▪ Stitch in the long, straight design lines first to hold the sandwich together.

2.15 ▪ Stitch in any other long passes and then short design lines to complete the rug.

YOU WILL NEED:

Towel: One cream-colored guest towel with even-weave strip

Fabric: 11″ × 4″ (28cm × 10cm) pink tulle; cotton fabric scraps: peach, yellow, green, blue polka dot

Needle: #80/12 jeans (sharp)

Thread: Lavender rayon machine-embroidery; cream sewing

Presser feet: Cording or open-embroidery; free-machine or darning

Cord: 2 yds. (1.85m) lavender pearl cotton

Stabilizer: 11″ × 4″ (28cm × 10cm) lightweight, tear-away

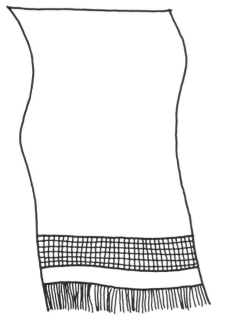

2.16 ▪ Towels with even-weave areas for decorating are available at craft stores.

Appliquéd and Embroidered Guest Towel

Guest towels have always been canvases for creative decorations, so much so that small fingertip towels are now available at craft and needlework shops. There's an open area on each towel that looks as though you must do counted cross stitches over the even-weave threads (Fig. 2.16), but don't let that limit you. This towel is decorated with appliqués covered with tulle, pearl cotton, and embroidery stitches.

Cut tiny ½″ (13mm) squares and rectangles of cotton fabric—the same fabrics used in the shower curtain—for the towel (Fig. 2.17). Once arranged over the open area of the towel, cover them with pink tulle. Pin the tulle down to keep the cotton fabrics from moving.

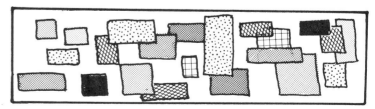

2.17 ▪ First cut up small scraps of many different fabrics and place them on the even-weave section.

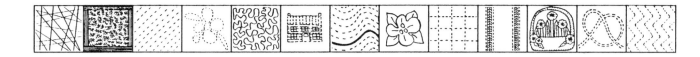

Use lavender rayon machine-embroidery thread in the needle, the towel color in the bobbin. Set your machine on free-machining by lowering the feed dogs and placing the darning foot or free-machine embroidery foot on the machine. Back the open area on the towel with tear-away stabilizer before stitching. Stitch up and back from the top of the area to about the middle and back again. When you reach the opposite side, stitch back, starting at the bottom of the area and stitching up to meet the other stitches. While stitching in zigzag lines across the area and back again, you've stitched the scraps in place (Fig. 2.18).

Change your machine to stitching with feed dogs up, a cording foot on. If you don't have one, then use an open-embroidery foot. Choose pearl cotton to couch over the tulle and zigzag stitches. (I chose the same color as the rayon machine-embroidery thread.) Set the stitching on stitch width 3, stitch length 3. Lay down the pearl cotton in an undulating, unstudied way and couch it in place (Fig. 2.19).

Then use the pearl cotton to make a raised satin stitch for a frame around the embroidered area (stitch width 3, stitch length shortened for satin stitch) (Fig. 2.20). Trim away the excess tulle.

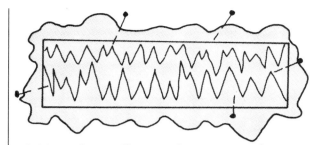

2.18 ▪ Place tulle over the scraps and freely stitch on top to hold the scraps in place.

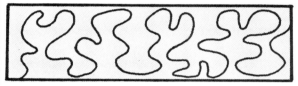

2.19 ▪ Lay pearl cotton on the tulle and couch it.

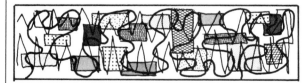

2.20 ▪ Couch pearl cotton around the edges to hold the tulle and clean up the edges.

YOU WILL NEED:

Towel: One rose guest towel with even-weave strip

Ribbons: Seven ¼″ (6mm) ribbons, each 10½″ (26.5cm) long: 2 light blue, 2 aqua, 2 yellow, 1 mauve; one ⅜″ (1cm) rose

Fabric: 10½″ × 4″ (26.5cm × 10cm) blue cotton

Needle: #80/12 jeans (sharp)

Thread: Rose rayon machine-embroidery; rose sewing

Presser foot: Open-embroidery

Fusibles: 2¼″ × 9½″ (5.5cm x 24cm) paper-backed web; 2¾″ × 9½″ (7cm × 24cm) fleece (optional)

Miscellaneous: Glue stick (optional)

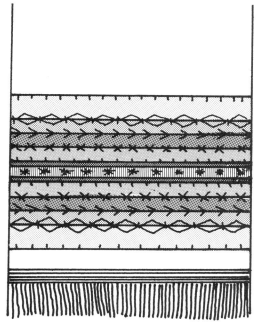

2.21 ▪ Attach grosgrain ribbon to cotton fabric by stitching it down with decorative stitches.

Ribbons and Decorative Stitches Guest Towel

The colors on this towel match those on the previous one. Collect ribbons and stitch them in place with decorative stitches (Fig. 2.21).

Arrange the colored ribbons in parallel lines on top of paper-backed fusible web, one ribbon directly against the next in this order: blue, aqua, yellow, rose, yellow, aqua, blue. Press them down.

Place the narrower mauve ribbon on top of the center rose ribbon. (Back the ribbon first with fusible web, then press onto the rose ribbon. Or use the optional glue stick instead: Rub glue stick along the back of the ribbon and press in place).

Remove the paper from the ribbons and trim off any web at the edges. Press them on the blue cotton, remembering to leave ½″ (1.3cm) margins at top and bottom.

Back the blue fabric with fusible fleece, if you wish. To bridge the ribbons, use symmetrical stitches, such as feather stitches. Stitch between the ribbons. Stitch stars across the center of the mauve ribbon.

Fold the blue fabric to fit inside the evenweave strip on the towel, leaving ¼″ (6mm) margins at top and bottom. Turn under the blue fabric on all sides. If you used fleece clip it back to the fold.

Apply the blue strip to the towel, using a decorative stitch.

3-D Appliqué Guest Towel

This flower appliqué is attached to Velcro and can be removed from the towel for laundering (Fig. 2.22).

Begin by drawing a simple flower shape on the back of five pieces of fabric (Fig. 2.23). Each flower is approximately 2″ (5cm) in diameter, though no two should be exactly the same. The fabrics are backed with other scraps and the outline completely stitched, trimmed, and the middle back snipped to turn the flower. Each flower shape is lightly

YOU WILL NEED:

Towel: One blue guest towel with even-weave strip

Fabric: Scraps of green, peach, yellow, and blue polka dot, for leaves, flowers; blue fabric, to cover Pellon

Needles: #80/12 universal; hand-stitching

Thread: Blue and green cotton machine-embroidery; blue sewing

Presser feet: General purpose; button sew-on

Miscellaneous: Handful of fiberfill; 3″ × 1½″ (7.5cm × 4cm) Velcro; 3½″ × 2½″ (9cm × 6.5cm) stiff Pellon; five ⅜″ (1cm) buttons, to coordinate with flowers

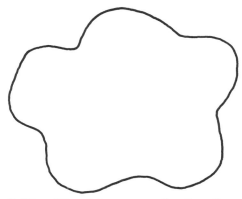

2.23 ▪ Use this pattern for five flowers.

2.24 ▪ Stitch from the outside edge to the center and back again to create petals.

2.22 ▪ Create a 3-D appliqué for a guest towel.

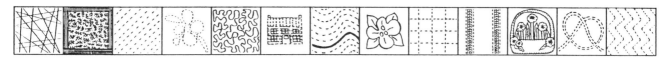

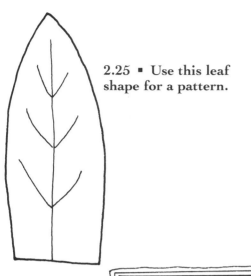

2.25 ▪ **Use this leaf shape for a pattern.**

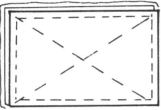

2.26 ▪ **Layer stiff Pellon between two pieces of cotton fabric.**

2.27 ▪ **Arrange leaves on the covered Pellon and stitch in place.**

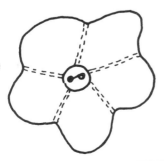

2.28 ▪ **Stitch buttons in place to attach flowers.**

filled with fiberfill. Hand-stitch the opening closed, then with the machine set on straight-stitching, stitch in lines with blue cotton machine-embroidery thread from the edges to the middle and back again to indicate petals (Fig. 2.24).

Next, stitch up six leaves (Fig. 2.25), turn, then fill with a bit of fiberfill. Stitch the veins in each leaf with green machine-embroidery thread.

Cover the Pellon piece, back and front, with blue cotton fabric the same color as the towel. Leave raw edges—they won't show (Fig. 2.26).

Then assemble the bouquet by first sewing down the six leaves to the blue backing piece (Fig. 2.27). Add half of the Velcro to the back of the Pellon.

Next, arrange the flowers over the leaves. Remember the arrangement, then remove all of them except the two underneath. Tack these in the centers with several zigzag stitches to hold them in place. Add the other flowers and stitch those in place, too.

Use small buttons for flower centers (Fig. 2.28). (Find colors to coordinate with the flowers.) Use glue stick to keep the buttons in place as you machine-stitch them down.

Sew the second half of the Velcro on the towel. The bouquet can now be removed for washing the towel, and the flowers can be washed as well, then smoothed out to dry.

Now how can you convince guests that these gems are, indeed, usable?

P R O J E C T   1 3

Sea and Shells Collage

If you love the excitement of making something truly original, then try this fabric collage. I've made fabric collages for years, but when anyone asks me how I do it, I'm hard-pressed to explain. I do know that I always have an idea of what I want (I never draw the design first), find the sheers and overlays I want to use, tear them into working pieces, then begin layering them. I use the machine to stitch layered fabrics in place, which gives the look of quilting, and sometimes I stitch directly on bridal tulle and apply this to the picture. If I stitch something down I don't like, I don't rip it out, I just stitch something opaque on top of it and keep going. That may remind you of oil painting, but from a few feet away the collages are mistaken for watercolors.

It's always easier to find a picture frame, then machine-stitch a piece to fit within. I did just that when I found one that looks wonderful with the bathroom colors I'd chosen. The frame is an antiqued aqua and gold one. The opening in the frame is only 3½″ × 4½″ (9cm × 11.5cm), so you won't be overwhelmed by this project; the frame size is 5½″ × 6½″ (14cm × 16.5cm). I

YOU WILL NEED:
Fabric: Transparent scraps of blue, teal, and green sheers (e.g., chiffon, organza, organdy, bridal tulle); opaque fabrics: 5″ (12.5cm) square of muslin, scraps of chartreuse and aqua
Needle: #90/14 jeans (sharp)
Thread: Gold metallic; clear monofilament; medium and light blue, light and dark aqua rayon machine-embroidery
Presser feet: Free-machine or darning; general purpose
Miscellaneous: Small frame with 3½″ × 4½″ (9cm × 11.5cm) opening; plywood to fit frame; vanishing marker; dressmaker's shears; three tiny sea shells; thick, tacky glue

2.29 ▪ **This collage of sheer fabrics is held in place with free-machine stitchery.**

planned an underwater scene of sheers and overlays to fit inside (Fig. 2.29).

You'll need several different sheer, transparent, and opaque fabric scraps for this picture. If you don't collect transparent fabrics as I do, then visit a thrift store and look for smoke-ring scarves, chiffons, and organza. (Buying there is often cheaper than fabric stores, and you can find inexpensive garments with fabrics unavailable in fabric stores.) I even buy shocking-pink fishnet stockings and pool table nets when I see them and always dig through gloves for suede, crocheted, or whatever I think I may use some time. Keep your eyes open and always look at things in a collage mode. But buy, also, at fabric stores when something glitzy, iridescent, or smashing appeals you. Fabric stores offer bridal tulle in a myriad of colors, and it's available in several widths. Purchase a quarter yard in several different blues and greens for this underwater collage.

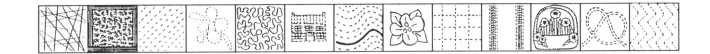

The colors used in this piece are aqua and teal along with several other blues, chartreuse, olive green, and lavender.

Place a base of dark aqua fabric on a backing of muslin. Draw around the opening of the frame with a vanishing marker, then straight-stitch ¼" (6mm) beyond that all around the aqua to hold the two pieces together and give you margins to work within. The fun begins when you start cutting the sheers into pieces. To prepare them, use a cut/tear method of snipping an edge, then pulling it through a scissors to create a fuzzy edge. Any rolled edges of chiffon scarves are torn off and saved, too as they are useful for dark, defining lines.

Use gold metallic, medium and light blue, as well as monofilament transparent thread.

Begin by layering three narrow (no wider than ½" [13cm]), uneven strips of chartreuse fabric (not a sheer) on the background (Fig. 2.30). Over this, layer sheers of different colors and sizes to look like the ocean depths of your dreams (Fig. 2.31). The layered sheers begin to look like a watercolor wash. In this collage, one light blue sheer of nylon looks like net and gives wonderful contrast to the plain fabrics already in place. Lavender rolled edges are placed in wavy lines across the picture. Then, over all this, stretch aqua bridal tulle to hold all the fabrics to the background. Pin it down in several places and take it to the sewing machine.

With the dark aqua thread in the needle,

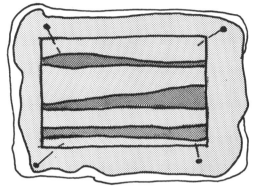

2.30 ▪ **First, place three strips of opaque fabric on the backing.**

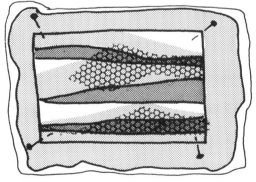

2.31 ▪ **Pin down strips of net or veiling for texture.**

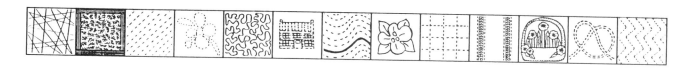

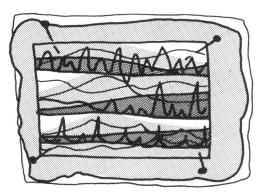

2.32 ▪ Stitch freely to hold the overlays in place and embellish the underwater scene.

freely stitch a jagged line of long and short zigzags across the top of the chartreuse scrap. Straight-stitch across below the center, but begin stitching up and back in long zigzags as you reach the other side. Then stitch across the bottom of the assemblage with the same thread, but in freely stitched scallops.

With light aqua in the needle, straight-stitch a wavy line across the top, middle, and bottom of the picture (Fig. 2.32).

Add texture to the picture by placing a narrow strip of frayed, dark teal chiffon across the picture, starting at the middle left side, curving down about 1" (2.5cm) and across to the other side. Stitch this down at the bottom edge with invisible thread.

Straight-stitch three wavy lines across the picture with gold metallic thread. Stitch around the entire collage on the same lines stitched when you attached the opaque background fabric. This holds all the wispy edges down.

Slip three tiny sea shells into the teal chiffon strip, and place a dot of thick, tacky glue behind each to be sure they stay in place.

Stretch the finished piece around a piece of thin plywood precut to fit the frame, and use thick, tacky glue to hold the edges to the plywood. After slipping it into the frame, tack the plywood in place.

Trust me, everyone who sees it will ask how it's made. The secret is ours.

Bedroom

I love the northwoods. I'm originally from Wisconsin, and once the sap starts flowing through the trees in spring, I can't wait to get in the car and head north to the lake we've frequented for over 30 years. Buffalo checks are perfect for that setting, so I imagined a bedroom in checks, fur, feathers, and felt by making pillows, a basket, and a wallhanging that could also be made as a table runner. Use these same ideas for a masculine bedroom in any setting.

Included in this chapter are the following projects: Summer Quilt, Leather Patch and Piece Pillow, Leather Ribbon Pillow, Leather Indian Basket, Ribbonwork Felt Wallhanging.

P R O J E C T   1 4

YOU WILL NEED:

Three sheets: One black-and-white checked or plaid flannel twin sheet, one white flannel twin sheet, one red percale queen sheet

Needle: #80/12

Thread: Red polyester sewing

Presser feet: General purpose; open-embroidery, braiding, cording, or Pearls N Piping

Yarn: One ball of Lily's red Sugar 'n' Cream

Miscellaneous: #1 or #2 safety pins; bonded batting, for binding

Summer Quilt

Help! I made a summer quilt and then everyone I told about it looked me straight in the eye and said, "Huh?"

"You know," I explained to anyone still listening, "a lightweight, three-layer quilt with a flannel sheet for batting?"

"Oh, right."

Hasn't anyone else ever heard of a summer quilt? Is it a Midwest term? Is it a family term? Must you have gray hair and remember Pearl Harbor to understand? I had to know. I searched my quilting library of books, then started calling experts around the country and asked them all the same question. It was a challenge.

I found out that a few people, young and old, do know the term (Oh, good, I didn't dream it!) and they aren't all from the Midwest. Friends from Texas know summer quilts, but theirs are only two layers thick. Most people in the know use theirs at vacation homes and all agree that summer quilts are a joy for crisp nights when heavy bedding is too much but you need a little something to keep you comfortable.

For this quilt I used a black-and-white buffalo-check flannel sheet for the top, a red percale sheet underneath, and between the two I placed a white flannel sheet. I couched

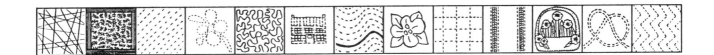

down cord over this sheet sandwich, quilting at the same time (Fig. 3.1).

Wash and dry all three sheets. (Flannel shrinks, and red bleeds. This proved true when I laundered them.)

Cut off 24" (61cm) from one side of the red sheet for binding the quilt later. To prepare the binding, cut the strip from top to bottom into four strips 6" wide (15cm) (Fig. 3.2).

Go on to prepare the checked sheet by cutting off one side or the other if the check design isn't even. Cut off top hems from all three sheets. (Don't just let out the hems, because the folds are impossible to press flat.)

Next, iron all the layers. Always press the two flannel sheets together as they have a tendency to stick together, which makes it easier for you when layering the sheets on top of the percale one. Safety-pin baste them together in the centers of checks. (This will make it easy to stitch along the sides of the checks.) If you have trouble closing the pins, use a spoon under the point of the pin.

First, fold the quilt sandwich in half to find the center square. Look at your checks and plan where you'll place your quilting lines. (This quilt is stitched down the side of every third square.) Using the sides as guides makes it easy.

Before quilting, straight-stitch across the top of the sandwich to hold it together.

Fill several bobbins with red thread so

3.1 ▪ **Couch down red cord every third square, to quilt.**

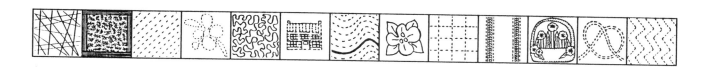

you'll have enough wound for the entire quilt. Instead of merely stitching the layers together, decorate the quilt at the same time, changing the black and white checks to a black-white-and-red plaid by couching Lily's red Sugar 'n' Cream at the sides of some of the checks.

Roll up the quilt sandwich the long way (pin the roll, if you wish), and place it to the right of the needle on the bed of the sewing machine. As you zigzag-stitch the yarn onto the quilt sandwich, the sheets feed off to the left, which keeps the bulk easy to maneuver.

If you feel the quilt is still too bulky to use my method, use this option: Roll both sides of the quilt to the middle. Quilt one side, beginning at the top center quilting line. Unroll and feed the quilt off the machine to the left as you complete the rows of quilting. After one side is quilted, turn the quilt around and complete the other side.

Set your machine on stitch width 3, stitch length 2.5. Tie a knot at the end of the yarn and place it under the presser foot. The presser foot I used has a large, high groove under it and the yarn is guided easily. Check the presser feet for your sewing machine. If you don't have one to accommodate a thick cord, you may want to use the Pearls N Piping foot, which is available through mail-order (see "Sources of Supplies"). The right presser foot always makes the job easier and faster—and the results more attractive.

As you zigzag over the yarn, keep smooth-

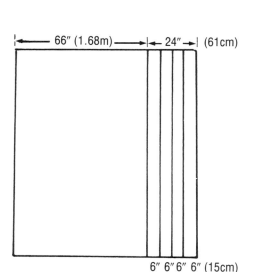

3.2 ▪ Cut off four 6″ (15cm) strips from the side of a queen-sized sheet to use as a binding.

ing and stitching till you get to the end of the line. Leave a tail of yarn at the bottom, then clip. Knot the end on the ball again and proceed with the second line. Finish all the lines, then rotate the sheet a quarter turn and stitch in the perpendicular lines to create a grid of red yarn (Fig. 3.3).

When finished, change to a general-purpose presser foot, and straight-stitch around the edge of the entire quilt to hold all the sheets together while binding them.

To bind the quilt, you can use any number of ideas: Use the extra fabric cut from the bottom sheet; buy and use red flannel; buy blanket binding at the fabric store. (This quilt is masculine-looking, so I nixed satin blanket binding.) You can also buy extra-wide, double-fold bias tape, though bias tends to ripple over time (Ugh!).

Let's use the red percale strips. With wrong sides together, press the binding strips in half the long way (Fig. 3.4). Measure the perimeter of your quilt and cut bonded batting in strips the same length, 1″ (2.5cm) wide.

Place the two binding edges at one side edge on the top of the quilt. Straight-stitch 1″ (2.5cm) from the edge down the length of the quilt. Use a seam guide for accuracy. Lay a 1″ (2.5cm) strip of batting on the edge, and fold over the binding around the edge and back to the stitching line (Fig. 3.5). Stitch the binding to the quilt by hand.

Or if you prefer to stitch the binding by

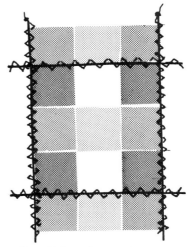

3.3 ▪ Couch by zigzagging over red cord.

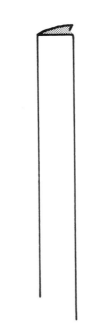

3.4 ▪ Fold and press the 6″ (15cm) binding strips the long way.

3.5 ▪ Stitch 1″ (2.5cm) from the edge and cover the edge with batting strip.

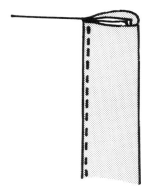

3.6 ▪ Turn folded edge over the quilt and stitch in place.

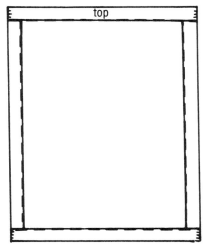

3.7 ▪ After binding the sides, bind top and bottom edges, then hand-stitch the side edges closed invisibly.

machine, attach the binding to the back side of the quilt first, straight-stitching 1″ (2.5cm) from the edge down the length of the quilt. Trim off the edge slightly, then pull the binding around and over the strip of batting on the top edge. Pin the folded edge slightly beyond the stitching line. Stitch down on the fold (Fig. 3.6). Complete two sides.

Add bindings to the top and bottom in the same way, but fold the binding inside at least 1″ (2.5cm) at each end. Hand-stitch the binding edges together invisibly (Fig. 3.7).

VARIATIONS:

1. Use sheets with predrawn lines, such as stripes, plaids, or checks; but instead of quilting by couching with yarn, use a decorative stitch on your machine. You'll be happy with a symmetrical stitch, especially if it crosses other lines of stitching. (Warning: This is much slower.)

When you plan stitching lines, leave areas no larger than about 6″ (15cm) square between lines of quilting. When quilting stripes, there is no need to quilt each line. Leave several inches (centimeters) between stitching lines.

2. Use a twin needle to quilt.

69   SUMMER QUILT

P R O J E C T   1 5

Leather Patch and Piece Pillow

I made this decorated pillow with one of the pillowcases in the buffalo-check flannel sheet set I bought to make the summer quilt (page 65).

To make one like it, cut the front of the pillowcase the same size as the pillow form (14″ [36cm]). The backing is prepared with a Velcro closure. To do this, cut the pillow back 2″ (5cm) wider than the front. Then cut the back in half lengthwise; each side is 8″ (20.5cm) wide. Fold one long edge under 1″ (2.5cm); fold the other over 1″ (2.5cm). Place strips of Velcro on the folded edges and stitch in place. Press the Velcro strips together and stitch above and below the Velcro on the folded edge. Go back and sew another row of stitches above and below the Velcro on the cut edges. These rows of stitches hold the pillow back together when the Velcro is open (see Figs. 1.63 and 1.64 on page 39).

Cut the pillowcase top to the size of the pillow form, 14″ (36cm). Decorate the top by layering suede, leather, and fur (Fig. 3.8). The pieces are sewn at the edges with black sewing thread, using the Teflon foot. Notice that I don't use a leather needle to sew leather. It's

YOU WILL NEED:

Fabric: Buffalo-check flannel pillow-case; red, white, gray, and black suede and leather scraps; pony-print Ultrasuede scraps; small fur piece

Needles: #100/16 jeans (sharp); sharp hand-sewing

Thread: Black polyester sewing; clear monofilament

Presser feet: Teflon; general purpose

Pillow form: 14″ (36cm) square

Miscellaneous: Beads; silver concho; found objects; tiny fur scraps (optional); leather strips; 12″ (30.5cm) Velcro strip; Household Goop or thick, tacky glue

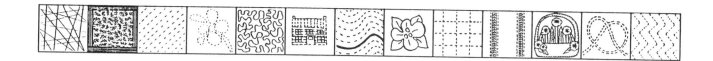

3.8 ▪ Layer leather and suede, then add decorations of beads, fur, leather, and suede strips.

not necessary to do so. Size #100/16 jeans needles are sharp and cut through many layers of leather and suede easily. If you have a problem, you can try #110/18 or #120/19.

To eliminate bulk, try my trick: First, I plan the top of the pillow by layering the leathers and suedes in an arrangement I find pleasing. Then I go back and use a dot of tacky glue on the backs of the leather pieces to hold them in place on the pillow-top fabric. If it is possible to trim away the covered leather underneath, I do it before pressing the glued leather in place.

When the top of the case is covered with patches, use clear monofilament thread to stitch a long piece of gray leather on the diagonal from one corner past the center. Stitch around the pillow top ¼″ (6mm) from the edge to hold the patches to the pillow front at the edges. Cut off the leather and suede beyond the flannel top.

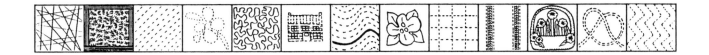

Place right sides of pillow front and back together. Sew around from the top slightly inside the stitching already there; then zigzag (or serge) the edges together for strength.

Change back to straight stitching. Shorten the stitches slightly and stitch 2–3 stitches diagonally across the pillow corners. Trim the corners to remove bulk before you turn the pillow to the right side.

Decorate the pillow top by gluing a piece of fur on top of the gray leather. (Use Household Goop or thick, tacky glue.)

To make the tassel at the top corner of the pillow, first thread up a long (at least 36" [.91cm]) piece of thread, double and knot it, and secure it to the top corner of the pillow. String beads, found objects, and fur scraps onto it. Skipping the last bead on the string, go back up through all the beads and objects again and secure the thread by stitching into the pillow-top corner. Don't cut off the thread.

Next attach two 18" (46cm) leather strips to the pillow by wrapping the same thread around the middle of the laces several times to hold them in place. Pull tight and anchor the thread. Clip off. Place a silver concho over the wrapped laces and pull the leather strips through both holes of the concho. Tie the strips together into a loop.

Use a second flannel buffalo-check pillowcase and more leather for the following pillow project.

YOU WILL NEED:

Fabric: Buffalo-check flannel pillowcase

Black, white, gray, and red leather and
suede scraps

13″ × 4½″ (33cm x 11.5cm) pony-
print Ultrasuede

12 white suede strips 13″ (33cm) long

5½″ × 13″ (14cm × 33cm) red
leather

18″ (46cm) red leather lace

Needle: #100/16 jeans (sharp)

Thread: Black polyester sewing

Presser feet: Teflon; general purpose

Pillow form: 12″ (30.5cm) square

Miscellaneous: Concho; beads; 10″
(25cm) Velcro strip

Leather Ribbon Pillow

Follow the directions in Project 15 to prepare the back of the flannel pillowcase, using
Velcro for the closure.

Cut the pillowcase top to the size of the
pillow form, 12″ (30.5cm). On the pillowcase
top, place the wide strip of red leather
slightly off-center (Fig. 3.10, next page).
Using the Teflon foot, sew across the top of
the pillow, securing the leather.

Sew the twelve white suede strips at the
top back of the pony-printed Ultrasuede,

**3.9 ▪ Buffalo checks and leather
decorative pillow.**

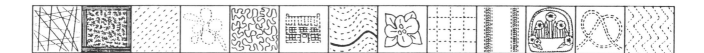

then center and sew this on the red leather (Figs. 3.11 and 3.12). Tie the leather lace around the leather and suede 5″ (12.5cm) from the top edge and slip the leather lace through the concho, using a square knot to tie it in place. Cut the pony print into long fringe below the tie.

Smooth the red leather over the pillow front and sew down at the bottom of the pillow front. With right sides together, sew the front and back squares together as you did the previous pillow. Turn right side out and insert the pillow form.

Add beads and knots on the leather laces (Fig. 3.9 on page 73.).

3.10 ▪ **First, stitch a wide strip of leather to the top of the pillow.**

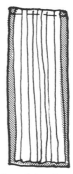

3.11 ▪ **Attach white leather fringe to the back of pony-printed Ultrasuede.**

3.12 ▪ **Sew fringe and Ultrasuede to top of the leather strip.**

YOU WILL NEED:

Fabric: 27" × 29" (69cm × 74cm) black grill cloth or heavy black interfacing

Scraps of suede and leather: red, black, white

27" × 29" (69cm × 74cm) black suede (this can be pieced)

Scraps of pony-print Ultrasuede

Needles: #100/16 jeans (sharp); hand-sewing

Thread: Black polyester sewing

Presser foot: Teflon, leather roller, roller, or walking foot

Miscellaneous: 2 yds. (1.8m) Craft Cord; concho; feathers; beads; suede and leather strips; leather lace; thick, tacky glue; newspaper; thimble

Leather Indian Basket

I can't resist the leather and suede "finds" at thrift shops when any skirt is 50 cents, any jacket $1.00. I buy scraps at the Tandy leather store and accept any donations by friends. (Thank you, Nancy.) It wasn't hard to find colors and textures to put together for this chapter when I discovered some leathers that looked different, but terrific, on both sides. The glove drawer at the thrift shop was a gold mine of white kid, and I found one black glove with beaded cutwork on the cuff (which I used at the top of the basket) (Fig. 3.13).

Even though I sometimes stitched through many layers of leather, I had no trouble when I used a #100/16 sharp (jeans) needle. Several presser feet can be used: leather

3.13 ▪ Leather and suede patched basket.

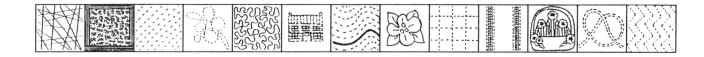

roller, roller, Teflon, or walking foot. For edge-stitching on leather, the Teflon foot is my favorite.

I used grill cloth for the basket lining. What is grill cloth? It is a heavily sized, open, black fabric used on stereo speakers, which is available at electronics stores such as Radio Shack. Of course, you may use stiff black interfacing, but grill cloth is almost like cardboard, and it makes construction easier.

First, cut out a pattern (Fig. 3.14) from newspaper for the basket. Then place the pattern over black grill cloth and cut it out.

Place this layer over the large piece of black suede and cut it out, or piece together black scraps to cover the grill cloth. Lightly glue the layers together where needed. Then take this to the sewing machine and attach the patches by straight-stitching at the edges of the scraps and stitch completely around the grill cloth edge. Trim off the leather back to the grill cloth.

Turn this over and piece the front on the grill cloth, arranging textures and colors attractively (Fig. 3.15). When finished, leave the edges of the leathers and suedes untrimmed. Fold up the arms of the cross to create the basket (Fig. 3.16). Sew the sides on the sewing machine as far as you can toward the bottom. This will leave slits at the bottom of the sides. Follow the edges of the leather pieces at the sides. You might add a patch or two to cover a straight seam line.

Wrap the Craft Cord with suede or leather

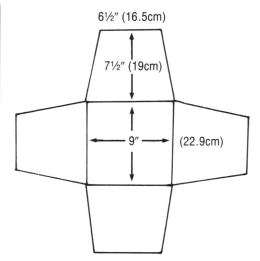

3.14 ▪ **Pattern for basket.**

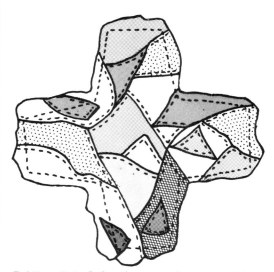

3.15 ▪ **Stitch leather patches to grill cloth.**

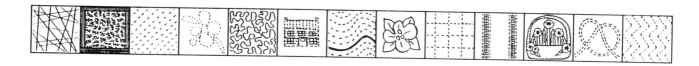

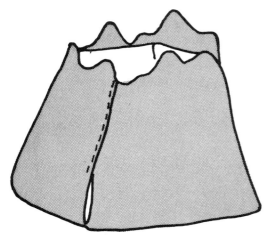

3.16 ▪ Fold up sides to overlap and stitch in place.

or both. Use dots of glue on the cord to hold the covering in place. Fold the cord in half and insert the two ends into one of the side slits at the bottom. Twist the cord and wrap it around the basket. Cut two slits, like buttonholes, into the middle side of the basket on the opposite side, and insert three suede strips into one slit and out the other. Tie strips around the wrapped cords to hold them in place. Cut two slits near the opening at the top on the side you started on and do the same to hold the cords in place on this side. Leave the loop of cord free. Glue inside the basket to keep the ends stable at the bottom.

Go back and add strips of leathers and suedes to make a tassel at the top of the basket at the slits over the Craft Cord. Add a concho over the cord and strips, and decorate under it with feathers and beads. To do this, dab glue on the bottom ends of feathers and slip them up under the concho. To attach beads, first string them on a long piece of doubled sewing thread, then hold both ends together to make a loop, leaving long ends of thread at each end. Tie the thread ends together with a square knot and then pull up both threads around the leather strips that hold the concho in place. Knot the thread ends together with a firm square knot and dab with glue. Clip the ends off.

Stitch beads to the basket, too—at the openings at the bottom of the basket to keep the sides together, or purely for decoration.

Ribbonwork Felt Wallhanging

Indian ribbonwork dates back to the 1700s. French traders offered silk taffeta ribbons in trade to the Native Americans, who at first used them as colorful additions to their garb. Designing with them was soon to follow. To do this, one ribbon was placed on top of another, then areas of the top ribbon were cut away to show the ribbon underneath. Geometry and nature were used as ideas for their designs, which were translated to ribbon. One half of the design was cut from one set of ribbons, the mirror image was cut from another set of ribbons, and both sets were stitched together. The appliquéd edges were turned under and stitched down.

I used a piece of newspaper 30″ × 50″ (76cm × 1.3m), folded it in half the long way, then folded it again the short way, and cut out a design on the long fold. Except for the initial design, which is drawn on the top layer of red felt, there is no more drawing—only measuring by the width of the presser foot. You can cut out circles using cups or glasses as guides (should your circles be smaller or larger than mine—do you care?), and painting a dowel end is less messy if you use a wide permanent marker. Time is saved

YOU WILL NEED:

Four felt pieces (red, white, gray, black): 15″ × 54″ (38cm × 1.4m) each

Black felt strip: 6″ × 54″ (15cm × 1.4m)

Needle: #80/12 sharp or universal

Thread: Clear monofilament; black sewing

Presser feet: Zipper; general purpose

Miscellaneous: Rotary cutter and mat; yardstick; 6″ x 24″ (15cm × 61cm) clear plastic ruler; 30″ × 50″ (76cm × 1.3m) newspaper; appliqué scissors; glue stick; pins; silver quilting pencil or vanishing marker; 24″ (61cm) heavy black cord, for hanging; ½″ × 17″ (13cm × 43cm) wooden dowel; two red wooden beads with ½″ (13cm) holes (optional); black permanent marker, for painting dowel ends

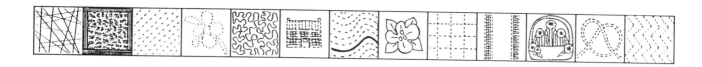

from beginning to end (and remember, too, because this is felt, I'm not turning under edges or satin-stitching them), so this is an example of quick construction if there ever was one (Fig. 3.17).

First cut black, red, gray, and white felt into the same size. Use a rotary cutter, mat, yardstick, and 6″ × 24″ (15cm × 61cm) clear plastic ruler to keep sides square.

Use newspaper for your pattern. Fold it in half the long way, 15″ × 50″ (38cm × 1.3m); then fold it the short way, 15″ × 25″ (38cm × 63.5cm). Draw, then cut out the design from the newspaper (Fig. 3.18, next page). Lay the center cutout aside and use the outline as the pattern. Open up the pattern and lay it over the red felt strip, leaving at least a 4″ (10cm) margin at the bottom below the cutout, and pin it in place. Draw the design on the red felt with a sharp, silver quilting pencil or vanishing marker. Remove paper pattern.

Next, place the red felt over the white and pin. Using clear monofilament thread, sew around the design ⅛″ (3mm) outside the pencil line. (The pencil line is the cutting line.)

You'll need short, sharp, pointed scissors for the next step. Appliqué scissors are ideal. Carefully cut only through the red top layer, cutting off the pencil marks, so the white layer shows. Next, layer the red and white felt design over the gray felt. Use a few pins to keep the fabrics from shifting. Then stitch

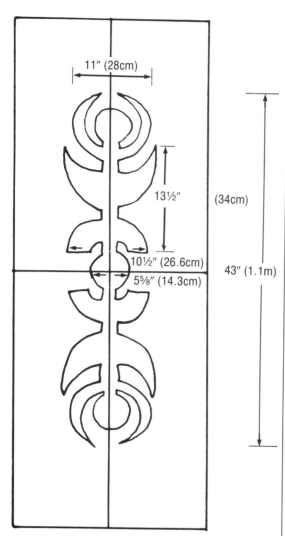

3.17 ▪ Simplified design for this wallhanging.

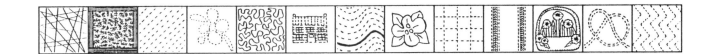

around on the white felt, ¼" (6mm) from the red design edge. (Don't measure—this is exactly my zipper foot's width with needle right. If your zipper foot is a hair narrower or wider, use it anyway. It'll be fine.) Again, cut back only the white felt almost to the stitching.

Place this stack of felt on the black background. Pin in place. Stitch as you did before, a zipper foot's width from the edge of the white felt, following the design. Cut through the gray to reveal the black backing.

Find the red felt cutout you laid aside. From it, cut out the three red circles, one 2¾" (7cm) in diameter for the center, two 2¼" (5.5cm) in diameter. Use a glue stick to attach these to the black background, then stitch around the circles close to the edge.

Measure and mark the edges of the wallhanging; finished size is 13" × 49" (33cm × 1.3m). Straight-stitch on those lines to hold the wallhanging edges together. Cut back to the stitching.

Cut two long strips of black felt, 1½" (4cm) by the length of the hanging. Place them on the top side of the hanging at the sides, matching cut edges. Bind the edges of the wallhanging, matching the edges of the binding and wallhanging at the top and along the side. Stitch, using the width of a general-purpose presser foot as a guide. Fold the felt binding around the edge. Stitch-in-the-ditch from the front, and then cut back to the stitching in back (Figs. 3.19 and 3.20).

3.18 ▪ Fold twice and cut once to make a mirror-image design for your own ribbonwork wallhanging.

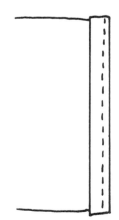

3.19 ▪ Stitch binding at each side edge.

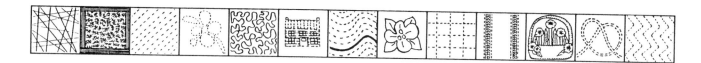

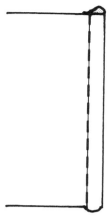

3.20 ▪ **Fold back around the edge and stitch-in-the-ditch to hold it in place.**

Cut another piece of felt the same width and slightly longer than the width of the hanging. Stitch the bottom edge as you did the sides, folding in the side edges when you reach them, then hand-sewing them together after completing the machine-stitching.

To make the casing for the ½″ (13mm) dowel hanger at top, fold under 1½″ (4cm) and stitch across near the cut edges (Fig. 3.21). Slip in the dowel. (Paint the ends black and add two large, red wooden beads at the ends, if you wish). Tie on cord for hanging.

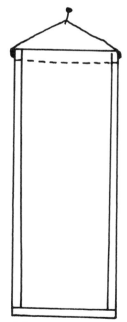

3.21 ▪ **Fold over the top edge to make a casing for a dowel.**

CHAPTER 4

Quilting/ Sewing Shortcuts

Try these shortcuts and hints to help you quick-quilt and -sew:

CAN'T-DO-WITHOUT'S

Rotary cutter and mat with grid and bias; 6″ × 24″ (15cm × 61cm) clear plastic ruler (use this for a T-square, too); glue stick; thick, tacky glue (leave it uncovered and it becomes even thicker); fusibles; silver quilting pencil; vanishing markers; water-erasable markers; seam guides; Hump Jumper, for stitching over thick seams; Fasturn, for tube turning; a dowel,

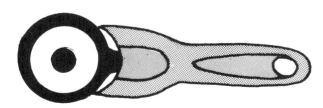

4.1 ▪ Rotary cutter.

4.2 ▪ Hump Jumper.

4.3 ▪ Fasturn.

4.4 ▪ A dowel shaped for pushing out corners and stuffing dolls.

to push out corners (one end is sanded flat like a paddle, the other is dull-pointed); and my stacks of boxes with thread, so I don't have to run out to buy thread every time I sit down to sew. (I buy monofilament thread, both clear and smoke, by the cone.)

The scissors I use most often are Fiskars 4″ pointed craft scissors and Mundial embroidery scissors. They cut all the way down to their tiny points. Also important to me are appliqué scissors (Gingher or Mundial). Most important of all are sharp cutting shears.

CLOSURES

Use Velcro for closures to save time when making a pillow. If you want a zipper closure, invisible zippers are the easiest to apply.

Use zippers-by-the-yard for odd sizes or large projects like duvet covers.

DECORATING PILLOWS AND QUILTS

A reversible pillow is like having two pillows, and it doesn't take much longer to sew. Decorate the pillow top and back differently, and leave an opening at one edge. Hand-sew closed.

If the pieces must meet perfectly, but you're afraid they won't, the best fudging trick I know is adding piping between the sections so being off a couple threads won't be noticeable (Fig. 4.5).

4.5 ▪ Slip piping between striped fabrics to fool the eye into seeing the stripes matching perfectly.

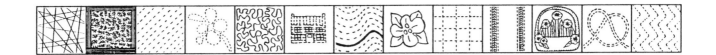

(But first try a walking foot, glue stick, basting tape, or fusible web strips to keep the seams in place while stitching.)

FABRIC

Use ready-mades whenever feasible: sheets for a summer quilt or duvet cover; decorated towels for rugs; or plain towels to decorate.

Use sheets for wide fabrics, but also look for extra-wide decorator fabrics in 90″ (2.3m) and 120″ (3m) widths. These are usually finish-treated, and the prints are straight on the fabric (not always true with sheets).

If a project doesn't fit across an available fabric width, check to see if you can avoid piecing by running your pattern the length of the fabric instead. (Be sure the print of the fabric is traveling in the right direction.)

Always buy more fabric than you need (don't we always?) to save possible trips to the store later. Also, fabric bought at one time will be from the same bolt and the dye lot won't vary. If you have leftovers, make napkins, wrapped baskets, patched pillows, small lap robes, even appliqués. Most of the accessories in this book are examples of projects made with small pieces of fabric.

Do you want only a hint of quilt batting? Use flannel yardage or sheets. Make bias the easy way (see Fig. 4.6–4.11).

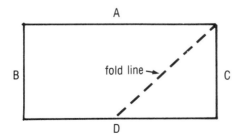

4.6 ▪ To cut bias, first fold up side C along dash line to meet side A.

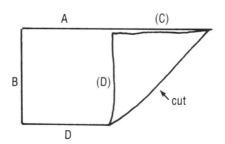

4.7 ▪ Cut along fold.

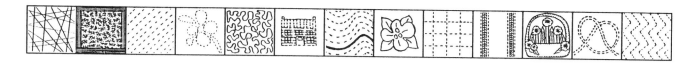

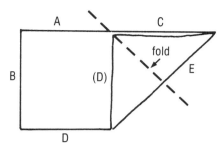

4.8 ▪ **Fold down from side C along dash line.**

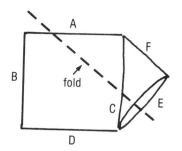

4.9 ▪ **Fold again on dash line parallel to side F.**

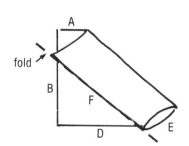

4.10 ▪ **Again, fold on dash line at F.**

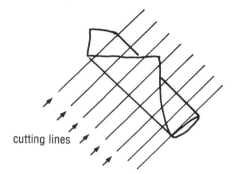

4.11 ▪ **Cut out bias strips perpendicular to the last fold line.**

FUSIBLES AND GLUES

Use fusibles whenever possible: fleece, webbing, bonds, and tear-away stabilizers. Use iron-on freezer paper for templates. Some fusible drapery tapes, webbing, and bonds can eliminate sewing completely—wow!

Sometimes use a glue stick or dots of thick, tacky glue in place of pins, or just because there are times when they are the best choice.

Even if you buy thick, tacky glue, there are times when you need the glue thicker than thick, so do what I do: Spoon out the amount of glue needed and leave it out for an hour or as long as it takes to thicken.

Household Goop is as thick as caulk and dries clear. It is the same as the product used by jewelry makers, E6000 (but cheaper). Buy it in the hardware store and use it whenever you're afraid bulky things will shift or slide before the glue is dry.

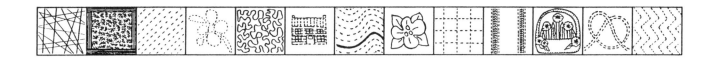

MEASURING

A rotary cutter mat with grid and bias lines is a must. So is a clear plastic ruler, 6″ × 24″ (15cm × 60.1cm).

When feasible, measure seam allowances with presser foot widths and de-centering needles (cut your fabrics to allow this seam allowance size). Lining up the presser foot edge at the edge of the fabric makes sewing a straight line easy and fast.

Use presser feet in combination with seam guides and screw-type seam guides for the bed of your machine when accuracy is a must.

To turn under a seam allowance easily, first stitch on the seam line, then turn under. This is especially helpful for ⅛″ (3mm) and ¼″ (6mm) hems.

PILLOWCASES AND PILLOW FORMS

If you need more filling in a pillow, wrap the pillow form with batting. Fill the pillowcase corners with handfuls of fiberfill.

When the pillow form is soft, cut the pillowcase the same size as the form. Then, when the ¼″ (6mm) seam allowances are sewn around the case, it reduces the pillowcase size and the form fits better. This doesn't work with thick rubber forms.

Round off pillowcase corners, or stitch 2–3 small stitches diagonally across them for a neater corner (see Fig. 1.40, page 30).

PIPING, WELTING, AND FRINGES

Always cover the piping and welting first, before attaching it to the edge of the pillow or quilt.

Attach piping, welting, or fringe to one side of the pillow at a time. After stitching the decoration to one side, pin to the other side, and using the stitching line as a guide, stitch the layers together slightly inside the line.

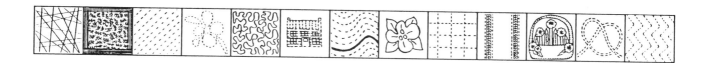

It's faster to buy covered piping, welting, and fringe by the yard, but weigh the cost—sometimes it's not worth it. Bite the bullet and make your own. The right presser foot makes covering piping and welting a breeze. Check Fasturn's method of making piping. It's super-fast.

QUICK-QUILTING CONSTRUCTION

Use safety pins for basting a quilt.

If possible, work in small, easy-to-manipulate sections. If you make a large quilt, divide it into sections and quilt the sections up to the seam allowances. Later sew the seam allowances together into the large quilt.

When quilting a large sandwich of fabrics, I pull my sewing machine table away from the wall and place a large piece of Masonite on it to keep the weight of the quilt from pulling the quilt away from the needle. It saves my shoulders.

Roll the quilt, then pin the roll together or use "bicycle clips" to hold it together. Fit the roll between the sewing needle and machine. Then, as you sew, the quilt feeds off the left-hand side, so you're not dealing with bulk (Fig. 4.12). Repin as you sew each section. Sometimes you don't have to pin at all.

Even if you've read that you must stitch in only one direction and start from the center and go out to each side, I've never listened to this. I stitch in whichever direction is the easiest to maneuver my quilt, and I've never been disappointed with the looks of the quilt.

4.12 ▪ **Place the quilt roll between needle and machine, letting the quilt feed off to the left.**

Though this won't make the quilt quicker, it's the hint my classes thank me for more than any other (they may be waiting for someone to give

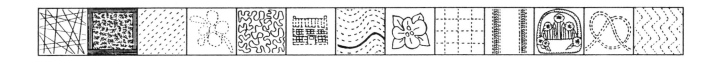

them permission): Never sit down at the machine and quilt from morning till night until you've finished the whole quilt. Instead, visually divide the quilt into sections. Make up your mind to quilt only one section a day. For example, when I make log cabin quilts, I quilt one row of squares each morning, then lay it aside till the next day and do another row. It may take me more than a week to quilt it, but when I'm done I can honestly say it was fun.

SPEED-QUILTING AND -SEWING

Quilt on printed lines on the fabric when you can.

Use striped fabric instead of piecing narrow strips of fabric together.

There are no puckers and pleats when you use a walking foot. In fact, know how to use all the specialty feet available for your machine. Use the best needle and thread for each job. And, most important, know your sewing machine!

Use your shirring foot or gathering accessory to gather ruffles, but zigzag over gimp to gather them if the fabric is heavy.

Load up multiple bobbins before beginning any project.

Use a serger for construction, even for decorating the fabric such as for rolled hems, gathering, and creating practical textures.

CHAPTER 5

What Size Will It Be?

When I make a quilt, I want it long enough to fit under the mattress at the foot of the bed and reach over my head at the top. Only then am I satisfied with the size. Someone once called that "wiggle room," a good word for it. I have to make one that size—a ready-made isn't available.

I have a "thing" about bedspreads, too. I want them to include enough fabric to reach the floor on three sides and fold under and turn over the pillows at the top. The fold is deep and the spread reaches to the head-board. I make bedspreads, too, because I'm never satisfied with the sizes of ready-mades. Isn't that why we all sew for our homes? We know, as sewing enthusiasts, we don't have to settle for just OK.

The charts that follow show standard sizes of beds, sheets, pillowcases, pillow forms, and tablecloths. That's a start. But if you want a longer than standard blanket, or deeper or shorter drop on a tablecloth, then make it the size you prefer.

If you want to be totally confused, check standard mattress measurements from more than one source. I consulted several different books and

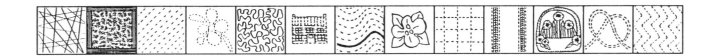

periodicals and arbitrarily chose the measurements that appeared most often on the charts (Fig. 5.1). When in doubt, measure the actual bed you're sewing for.

Standard bedding sizes are as follows:

MATTRESS

6-year crib	27″ × 52″	(68.5cm × 1.3m)
Twin	39″ × 75″	(99cm × 1.9m)
Double	54″ × 75″	(1.4m × 1.9m)
Queen	60″ × 80″	(1.5m × 2m)
King	76″ × 80″	(1.9m × 2m)
Calif. King	72″ × 84″	(1.8m × 2.2m)

FLAT SHEET

27″ × 36″	(68.5cm × .9m)
66″ × 96″	(1.7m × 2.4m)
81″ × 96″	(2m × 2.4m)
90″ × 102″	(2.3m × 2.6m)
108″ × 102″	(2.7m × 2.6m)

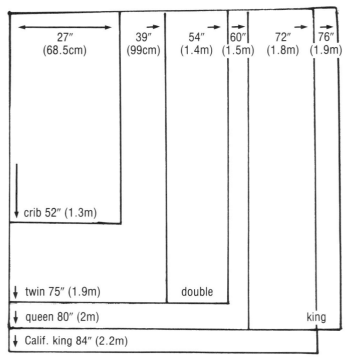

5.1 ▪ **Mattress sizes.**

The standard drop for beds is 21″ (53.5cm).

BED PILLOW SIZES

Standard	20″ × 26″	(51cm × 66cm)
Queen	20″ × 30″	(51cm × 76cm)
King	20″ × 36″	(51cm × 91.5cm)

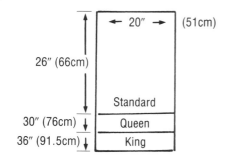

5.2 ▪ **Bed pillow sizes.**

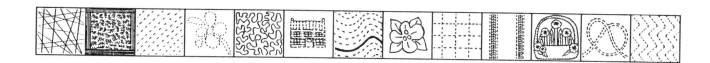

Decorative Pillow Forms: Decorative standard square pillow forms are 12″ (31cm), 14″ (36cm), 16″ (41cm), 18″ (46cm), 20″ (51cm), 26″ (66cm), 30″ (76cm). Odd shapes and sizes are available at decorator fabric shops.

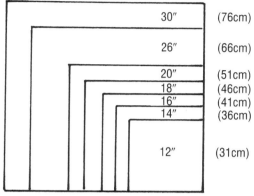

5.3 ▪ Decorative pillow form sizes.

Tablecloths: Standard drop lengths are short for everyday use, 10″ (25.5cm) to 12″ (30.5cm), or long to reach the floor, approximately 29″ (73.5cm) for decorator tables.

Standard tablecloth sizes for everyday use:

52″ × 52″   (1.3m × 1.3m)
52″ × 70″   (1.3m × 1.8m)
60″ × 84″   (1.5m × 2.2m)
60″ × 120″ (1.5m × 3m)
60″ × 144″ (1.5m × 3.7m)
70″ round   (1.8m)
90″ round   (2.3m)

Standard shower curtain size:
72″ × 72″ (1.85m × 1.85m).

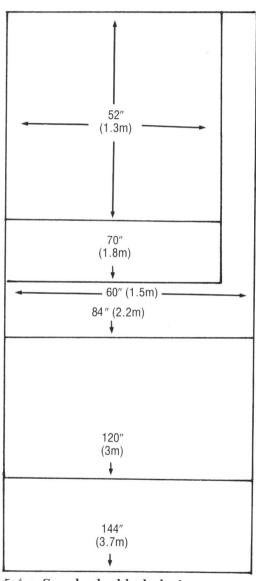

5.4 ▪ Standard tablecloth sizes.

Now get out a tape measure, pencil, and notebook. If you can measure, you can decorate.

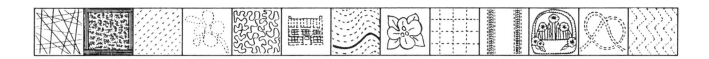

AFTERWORD

When I sew, I love to experiment. I'm inspired by fabrics and threads, and when I start designing projects, it's always "What if . . . ?" Once I begin asking myself questions, one idea leads to another and another, and soon I have a stack of experiments on my sewing table. I won't use many of them; they're just part of the progression from first spark to success.

I've included some of those successes in this book. Start with them as written, or use the projects as a jumping-off place for your own experiments by changing the colors, fabrics, threads, and stitches. That's what makes home decor sewing fun. It's also fun saying, "I made it myself."

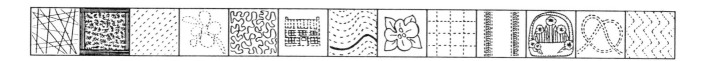

BIBLIOGRAPHY

Allen, Alice. *Sashiko Made Simple.* Hinsdale, IL: Bernina of America, 1992.

Black, Lynette Ranney, and Linda Wisner. *Creative Serging for the Home.* Portland, OR: Palmer/ Pletsch Associates, 1991.

Brown, Gail. *Gail Brown's All-New Instant Interiors.* Radnor, PA: Chilton Book Co., 1992.

Cairns, Pat. *Contemporary Quilting Techniques.* Radnor, PA: Chilton Book Co., l991.

Coleman, Ann. *Quilting New Dimensions,* London, England: Batsford Ltd., 1989.

Colvin, Maggie. *Pure Fabrication.* Radnor, PA: Chilton Book Co., l985.

Fanning, Robbie, and Tony Fanning. *The Complete Book of Machine Quilting.* Radnor, PA: Chilton Book Co., 1980.

Finishing Touches. Radnor, PA: Chilton Book Co., 1992.

Hallock, Anita. *Fast Patch.* Radnor, PA: Chilton Book Co., 1989.

Hargrave, Harriet. *Heirloom Machine Quilting.* Lafayette, CA: C & T Publishing, 1990.

Johannah, Barbara. *Continuous Curve Quilting: Machine Quilting the Pieced Quilt.* Menlo Park, CA: Pride of the Forest, 1980.

Kinser, Charleen. *Sewing Sculpture.* NY: M. Evans and Co., Inc., 1977.

Lehman, Bonnie, and Judy Martin. *Taking the Math Out of Making Patchwork Quilts.* Wheat Ridge, CO: Moon Over the Mountain Publishing, 1981.

Moore, Nancy. *Machine-Quilted Jackets, Vests, and Coats.* Radnor, PA: Chilton Book Co., 1991.

Reader's Digest Complete Guide to Sewing. Pleasantville, NY: Reader's Digest Association, Inc., 1976.

Roberts, Sharee Dawn. *Creative Machine Art.* Paducah, KY: American Quilter's Society, 1992.

Rostocki, Janet. *Sashiko for Machine Sewing.* Dayton, OH: Summa Design, l988.

Scott, Toni. *The Complete Book of Stuffedwork.* Boston, MA: Houghton Mifflin Co., 1978.

Short, Eirian. *Quilting Technique, Design and Application.* London, England: Batsford Ltd., 1983.

Singer Reference Library. *Sewing Projects for the Home.* Minnetonka, MN: Cy DeCosse Inc., 1991.

———. *Sewing for the Home.* 1988.

———. *More Sewing for the Home.* 1987.

Slipcovers and Bedspreads. Menlo Park, CA: Lane Publishing Co., 1983.

Solvit, Marie-Janine. *Pictures in Patchwork.* NY: Sterling Publishing Co., Inc., 1977.

Wagner, Debra. *Teach Yourself Machine Piecing and Quilting.* Radnor, PA: Chilton Book Co., 1992.

Wormleighton, Alison, ed. *Soft Furnishings for the Home.* NY: Simon & Schuster, Inc., 1985.

SOURCES OF SUPPLIES

(so that you can keep burrowing)

Aardvark Adventures, Box 2449, Livermore, CA 94550 (800/388-ANTS). A wonderful collection of unique threads (distributor of Natesh rayon machine-embroidery thread), beads, bells, kits, or you name it, for all needlepeople. There is a fantastic, free newsletter, "Aardvark Territorial Enterprise," when you become a customer. (Or subscribe for $12 with U.S. zip code; $15 foreign.) Catalog $2 (refunded with first order).

Buffalo Batt & Felt Corp., 3307 Walden Ave., Depew, NY 14043 (716/683-4100, ext. 8). Fiberfill, quilt batt, and pillow forms. Brochure with samples ($1 refundable).

Cabin Fever Calicos, P.O. Box 550106, Atlanta, GA 30355. Quilt books, notions, fabrics, batting. Send for their fabric swatches and you'll be entertained for hours.

Clotilde, Inc., 1909 SW First Ave., Ft. Lauderdale, FL 33315 (800/722-2891). Generic sewing machine feet, pearls and piping foot, threads, books, videos, needles, and notions. Free catalog.

The Crowning Touch, 2410 Glory C Rd., Medford, OR 97501 (503/772-8430). Makers of Fasturn turning tools and Fastube sewing foot, hi/low adaptor. LSASE.

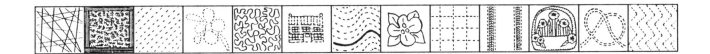

The Fabric Center, 488 Electric Ave., P.O. 8212, Fitchburg, MA 01420-8212 (508/343-4402). Discounts on most major decorator fabrics. Free brochure; 164-page catalog $2.

Fairfield Processing Corporation, 88 Rose Hill Ave., P.O. Box 1157, Danbury, CT 06813. Products include four types of fiberfill (Poly-Fil, Poly-Fil Supreme, Crafter's Choice, and EZ Stuff), four bonded and two needlepunch battings in a variety of sizes, pillow forms in firm and down-like softness, pellets for use as weighted stuffing material, and a line of patterns. Call 800/243-0989 to locate the nearest retail store in your area.

G Street Fabrics, Mail Order Service, 12240 Wilkins Ave., Rockville, MD 20852 (301/231-8960). Mail-order fabrics and custom service. They'll send swatches.

The Green Pepper, 3918 West First Ave., Eugene, OR 97402 (503/345-6665). Recreational fabrics, battings, hardware, and zippers. Catalog $2.

Home-Sew, Dept. QQ1, Bethlehem, PA 18018 (215/867-3833). Sewing notions, laces, trims, buttons, zippers, ribbons, some fabrics. Free catalog.

Kaye Wood Publishing Co., P.O. Box 456, West Branch, MI 48661 (800/248-KAYE). Quilting supplies, specialized tools, videotapes, and books. Catalog of quilting supplies $1.

Keepsake Quilting, P.O. Box 1459, Meredith, NH 03253 (603/253-8731). Send for their catalog, which includes notions, fabrics, books, and batting.

Kunin Felt—a Foss Mfg. Co., 380 Lafayette Rd., P.O. Box 5000, Hampton, NH 03842 (800/233-3358). Manufacturer of 100% polyester colored felt. Wholesale, but they will answer your questions and direct you to stores in your area that sell their felt.

Madeira Marketing, Ltd., 600 East Ninth St., Michigan City, IN 46360 (800/275-9003 or 219/873-1000). High-quality yarns, threads, and flosses. LSASE.

Nancy's Notions, Ltd., P.O. Box 683, Beaver Dam, WI 53916 (800/833-0690). Books, videos, notions, glues, machine accessories, wide-width decorator fabrics, fusibles, Ultrasuede, and Ultrasuede scraps, pearls and piping foot. Free catalog.

National Thread & Supply, 695 Red Oak Rd., Stockbridge, GA 30281. Name-brand sewing supplies and notions. Free catalog.

Newark Dressmaker Supply, P.O. Box 20730, Lehigh Valley, PA 18002-0730. Pleating and shirring tapes, decorator fabrics, sewing notions, decorative threads, trims, and laces. Free catalog.

Oregon Tailor Supply, P.O. Box 42284, Portland, OR 97242 (800/678-2457). Notions and threads. LSASE.

Pacific Fabrics Shop at Home, P.O. Box C3637, Seattle, WA 98124 (800/446-6710). Lampshade frames, fabrics, notions.

Quilters' Resource, Inc., P.O. Box 148850, Chicago, IL 60614. Lamés, threads, kits, buttons, and braids you won't see anywhere else.

Quilting Books Unlimited, 1911 W. Wilson, Batavia, IL 60510 (708/406-0237). Large selection of quilt-related books. Catalog $1.

Quilts & Other Comforts, Box 394, 6700 W. 44th Ave., Wheat Ridge, CO 80034-0394. Publishers of *Quilter's Newsletter Magazine* and *Quiltmaker*, their catalog contains fabric, patterns, templates, books, and kits. Catalog $2.50.

Sew Art International, P.O. Box 550, Bountiful, UT 84010. Unusual threads.

Sew/Fit Co., 5768 West 77th Street, Burbank, IL 60459 (800/547-ISEW). For local or Canadian calls—708/458-5600. Notions, cutting tools, and mats. Free catalog.

Speed Stitch, 3113 Broadpoint Drive, Harbor Heights, FL 33983 (800/874-4115). Sulky rayon and metallics, invisible threads, machine-embroidery supplies, and kits. Catalog $3 (refundable with order).

Treadleart, 25834 Narbonne Ave., Lomita, CA 90717 (800/327-4222). Decorative and utility machine threads, notions, books, patterns. Bimonthly magazine. Catalog $3.

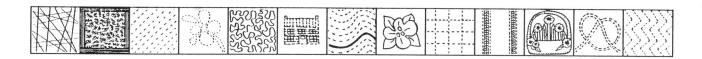

INDEX

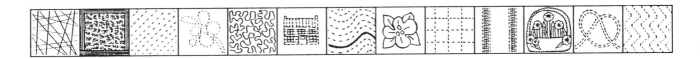